TO MATTIE,

In memory of our old-fashioned games" which brought us together.

Margaret

ANCHOR BOOKS

POETRY LIFE

First published in Great Britain in 1995 by
ANCHOR BOOKS
1-2 Wainman Road, Woodston,
Peterborough, PE2 7BU

HB ISBN 1 85930 293 9
SB ISBN 1 85930 298 X

Foreword

Anchor Books is a small press, established in 1992, with the aim of promoting readable poetry to as wide an audience as possible.

We hope to establish an outlet for writers of poetry who may have struggled to see their work in print.

The poems presented here have been selected from many entries. Editing proved to be a difficult and daunting task and as the Editor, the final selection was mine.

The poems chosen represent a cross-section of styles and content. They have been sent from all over the world, written by young and old alike, united in the passion for writing poetry.

I trust this selection will delight and please the authors and all those who enjoy reading poetry.

Glenn Jones
Editor

CONTENTS

THE GIFT OF FRIENDSHIP

What gift can I give more precious than gold
That will never tarnish wear out or grow old
And becomes even dearer as long years go by
It's the gift of true friendship a bond you tie
For a friend is someone who is always there
To share all our problems and lessen our care
To weather each storm and still there remain
To share laughter and pleasure teardrops and pain
Friendship is a priceless gift beyond all measure
It cannot be bought it's life's richest treasure
Friendship brings comfort an outreaching hand
It lends an ear and a heart to understand
Each others problems with the power of perception
When in need of sympathy, kindness and affection
By each other you stand through the highs and lows
And so your friendship strengthens and grows
Friendship is caring, being thoughtful and kind
Nothing quite like it in the world you'll find
The freedom of knowing you can say without fear
The words your friend may not want to hear
Sound in the fact that both of you will
At the end of it all be good friends still
It can't be gift wrapped or dressed with a bow
It comes from the heart and freely does flow
A gift that when given you can share every day
And it grows all the more when given away.

C A Burnup

PRINCE CHARLES

Prince Charles is really in a mess
He's not being helped by the daily press
He should have saved humiliation
By not making his revelation
Camilla could have kept her distance
By putting up a good resistance
Maybe Charles should not be King
If he cannot honour his wedding ring
Camilla now has got divorced
Was it her choice or was it enforced
Her marriage to Charles would not be right
Unless he gave up the throne in desperate plight
But William and Harry would surely suffer
Without their own devoted mother
Heirs to the throne they would still be
So give them their right of destiny.

Marguerite Rose

TO BE USED OR NOT TO BE

Royalty are hunted by:
The media yet should
Understand they have a living
To get

What be the difference
In hunting the fox
If be more understanding
Of the situation could
Result in less royal
Regret.

Roma Taylor

2

FIRE CAT

Listen to the sound
Listen to the sound.
Of the fire, crinkling, cracking.
The cat's throaty purr
In tune with the flame.
Listen to the sound,
Of the ashes and the beast.
No more related than wind and fur,
Than ghost and priest.
Listen to the sound
Of wet wood spit.
Beside the stone
Where the cat chose to sit.
Red turns to ruby.
Ruby to black.
The fire cat rolls over
Like a burnt umber sack.
Content Warm Fed.
Stretched without guard.
A satisfied victim of a medieval rack.
Listen to the sound
Purring
As fire black turns
To ash grey.
A charcoal shadow stalks
And kills
Its cold prey.

Peter Drahony

THE RUNAWAY

She wandered through the busy streets - she'd run away from home.
She wished she'd never been so daft - she felt so much alone.
The people rushing here and there with never time to speak,
It was all most bewildering - she felt so young and meek.

She'd come up from the country with ideas oh so plain
Of London with its streets of gold, but it wasn't quite the same.
She realised now just what she'd lost - the home she'd left behind.
The family that loved her. She wondered if they'd cried,

When they had found her bedroom, so empty and so bare.
She regretted her decision but thought 'P'raps they won't care.'
But deep inside she knew they would be really devastated.
The realisation that she'd hurt them was something that she hated.

When this was planned it seemed to her a brilliant idea.
London and its glitter was calling her up here.
But now she looked around her. The truth was very clear.
The dirty streets, the smoky air - what was she doing here?

She thought with longing of her home - in self-pity she could wallow.
She knew that she could go back home if her pride she would but swallow.
The darkness started falling and she was very scared.
A cardboard box could be her home. There was no one here who cared.

Except her family that she'd left as if they didn't matter.
She thought again of home right now and her baby brother's chatter.
It soon would be his bedtime - he would miss his bedtime story.
He loved to hear her read to him of dragon fights so gory.

Just then a hand fell on her arm - a voice spoke in her ear.
'You silly girl - we've found you - now please come home my dear.'
Her father's voice, her mother's arms - she couldn't just believe
They'd searched and searched and found her - oh what a great relief.

Never again would she think it fun to run away from home.
For all its size - in London you could be so much alone.
The train pulled out and off it sped, past villages and farms.
But she was safe upon that train within her mother's arms.

Jennie Rippon

LOVE'S DEATH

Turn out the lights.
Lock the door.
I am alone
For evermore.

Pull down the blinds.
Shun the 'phone.
I am at home now
All alone.

Tell everyone
I am done.
No more alive.
My life has gone.

Now evening comes.
Dark does fall.
I am without
My love's sweet call.

No moon no star.
No more sun.
Turn out the lights
My day is done.

Ray Nurse

THE LOOKING GLASS

Looking through the window
What visions do I see?
Do you know what I know?
Could it be that you are me?

Are you just my image,
A reflection in the glass?
A ghost that's come to haunt me?
Or just a person from the past?

What lies beyond the window?
Beyond the bricks, beyond the walls?
The image tries to answer me,
But there's silence in his calls.
I'll destroy this window break it set him free,
But, no, I cannot do this, for the image, it is me!

Steven Casey

TODAY IS THE DAY

Today is the day the lord took my dad away
Today is the day I wish I could wipe away
Today is the day when your life came to a halt
Today is the day when we all felt a jolt
Today is the day when I felt grief
Today is the day when you felt relief
Today is the day when you passed away
Today is the day I wish never came your way
Today is the day when I remember the smiles you could never hide
Today is the day when I remember with pride
Today is the day when I lost a friend
Today is the day when I realised all good things must come to an end!

Diane A Bell

CAR BOOT

My prison's small and black
The lid pressed down on my back
Can't move, can't force the latch
But my mind's exploding
Outside I hear the cries
Our freedom he denies
My peace of mind is lies
Madness creeps up on me.
       Boyfriend locked in car boot while girl is raped
       That'll be the headlines for Thursday.
Now panic's the only thing
Insanity advancing
What's that song we used to sing
Let's keep my head together
Try keep my mind on track
But oxygen's my lack
My lights fade to black
Is this my ending? . . .

Ian J Pettit

A FELINE FEEDING SCENE

Tensely watchful, eyes unwinking,
Ears erect at once to hear,
Paws of velvet stiff and ready -
Object of desires appear!

Springing forward, arched, excited,
Feigned affection briefly share,
Dainty nibbling, deftly cleansing -
Softly rolled, a ball of fur.

Rosemary Y Vandeldt

OUR TINA

Head tilted to one side,
Bushy tail wagging,
Eyes shining alert and bright
Pink tongue hanging

A friendly paw, a lick on the face
A welcome when you would appear,
This picture we'll always carry of her
One who loved so dear.

So many happy memories
She was such a gentle creature
Even the tiny birds in the trees
Were to her a happy feature.

She'd know when the biscuit plate was near
Even though she was lying asleep
Her head would rise, her ears would cock
'Twas a secret you never could keep.
She'd plead so nicely, 'Yes I am here
Please don't forget about me
I'll help you clear the plate' she'd say
And who could resist her plea.
Those lovely eyes would fix their gaze
With just the right expression
Such a pathetic look, would appear,
It certainly made an impression.

Many tears were shed
The day she died
It was hard to say good-bye
But the memories we carry around today
Are of a happy dog in the sky.

J Lawrie

MY FAMILY FOR ALL TIMES

The turkey rests, all else is done
United we rise to greet our mum.
Now dad and sis, went out to war
And baby Bob n'er his dad saw.
Mum took the lead, she made a plan
To help the family, and our gran.
When news was grim and dad seemed lost
She cheered us up but at what cost!
Then dawned the day, the letter came
Dad's on his way, the war's near done.
The cheering soon had died away
Dear mum she faced another day
A day of hope, a day so warm
The day our little Ted was born.
So after that we soldiered on
And wasn't long 'fore sis came home.
Though war was o'er and fighting done
Another began to save our mum
For burdened she with pain and strife
So long both husband and a wife
She fell so ill, was touch and go
We all cried mum we love you so.
But mum was brave, she fought with will
In hospital bed I see her still.
So come in mum, it's Christmas time
Let's celebrate with food and wine
And from our table let's make a plea

Dear God - preserve our family.

Cyril Saunders

CHRISTIE JAYNE

You never got to say hello
Or even make a sigh
Just a kiss and cuddle
And we quickly said goodbye

You looked so sweet and peaceful
With your brother's little nose
Your crumpled red hair, long fingers
And perfect little toes

We didn't have long together
Because you couldn't stay
We don't know the reason why
You had to go away

We'll never get to watch you grow
Or even see you smile
Or see how fat you had got
In just a little while

Your mum and dad they miss you
And they always will
They've been robbed of their memories
And time is standing still

I want to say we all love you
You are part of our family
It's just so sad your mum and dad
Didn't get to bounce you on their knee

One day we'll all meet up together
And then perhaps we'll know
Why you didn't stay with us
Why you had to go

Goodbye you little sweetheart
Sleep well and never fret
I'm sorry we can't hold you again
But I'm very glad we met.

G Rollins

SKIN DEEP

As I look into the mirror,
I scrutinise my face, I check to see,
If all my bits are perfectly in place,
Two eyes, a nose, a little mouth,
A brow and double chin? The fact that
I like cream cakes is the reason for
This sin!
So what do people think of me?
Staring in my direction, what do they see?
Have I got crows feet or are they
Laughter lines? When I smile, is it
My teeth or my T-zone that shines?
Are my features even or do they
Go all conky? Is my nose
Straight or maybe slightly wonky?
Oh! I give up, I don't care anymore,
My eyes are heavy and my brain's
Getting sore!
I'm going to bed to get a few
Hours sleep!
After all who cares anyway
Beauty's only skin deep!

Michelle Hattam

LUV 'N' STUFF

I look out my window, what do I see?
A beautiful man looking at me!
Eyes of azure blue, topaz hair
I look, I wonder, I stare.

Do you see me I think not.
Do you know what you have got?
Panache, pazzazz, an air of grace
Did I put that smile upon your face

I hope I did and what is more
Marvellous things I have in store
Fun, flirtations, laughter, joy,
For the gorgeous man who looks like a boy.

I guess I have blown my cover
So with my lips I will smother
This card with kisses divine
Lots of luv from your valentine.

Janette Homer

I

I learnt to read
At great speed

I learnt to write
Over night

I learnt to spell
Ever so well

And in everything else
I've learnt to excel.

Sonia Sweet

THE CIRCLE LINE

Not a soul, or a person to fill
The seats on the subway train.
I sit alone, spying through the murky print-stained windows,
The chasing carriages.
Hanging from the roof, a line of redundant
Springed handles
Waggle, like tails of lambs at a trough.
The metal worm meanders through dirt city.
Slowing, the engine guides us between two
Desolate platforms.
The doors slide open.
Nothing stirs: The doors close.
With a hiss and a rude squeak the train eases away.
Even as I watch,
The dirt congregates in every crevice.
Orders are issued from poster-boards,
Positioned impolitely to glare at me.
I read them mechanically
Over and over. Preying on my ignorance,
They all clamour to drain the juice
From my pockets.
Escape:
The trees flash by in a flurry of greens
And blossom.
I can almost hear the cry for moisture in the
Languid, musty heat of the suburbs.
A voice speaks only to me as it imparts
Cracked information over the tannoy:
Is this the end of the line?

Anthony Hodder

LIMERICK 1995

There was a young lady of Ramsgate,
Who relished a fine chop on her plate.
One day she heard a bleat
From the cargo of meat.
And thereafter all flesh did she hate.

Meg Pybus

BEAUTY

What is beauty?
A philosopher may ask.
Is beauty skin deep?
Beauty is in the eye of the beholder.

Beauty as a simile.
Is beauty like a box of chocolates?
Can you hold it?
Can you feel it?
Can you see it?
Can you hear it?
Can you smell it?

Beauty is all around us.
Beauty is nature.
Beauty lives and breathes.
Beauty is young.
Beauty is old.
Beauty is vitality.
Beauty is individuality.
Beauty is to be celebrated!
Beauty is life!

Laura Price

PAST THE SELL-BY DATE

I'm finding it harder as years go by,
To look in the mirror and not heave a sigh,
At a certain angle I'll put my face,
Where the light will help, strategically placed,
Where are the roguish, twinkling eyes?
Buried in bags that reach to my thighs,
Where is the pert nose that boys did admire?
One drink too many has set it on fire,
Where are the lips like strawberry dunes?
Wrinkled and sucked in like great bags of prunes,
The smooth, translucent skin of shimmering hue,
Never again will look like the dew,
Instead, it's a road map of England and Wales,
With a special route march along Yorkshire Dales,
Oh give me some comfort, a face-lift or two,
When the tractor has lifted me out of the loo,
I wish that I was younger and fitter,
When the size of my bra did not raise a titter,
Rock 'n' roll, flower power, I've had my thrills,
I now scour the paper for potions and pills,
Something to magically bring back my youth,
Then folks won't say, 'She's long in the tooth,'
But I must admit if not seen for a while,
A stranger will say with a dawning smile,
'Aren't you?' 'Yes I am,' 'My God, you've not changed,
I always said you were top of the range,'
I smile in elation, the sun's out at last,
The warmth taking over with a blast from the past!

Annie Storey

TURN BEAUTY INSIDE OUT!

Beauty and the Beast
Harmony of sound!
But, would it not be better
The other way round!
Has not the beast more beauty than
The *beauty*?
Turn beauty inside out.

Look like the flower but be the serpent
Beneath!
Would the contrary so readily appease?
Turn beauty upside down!

If beauty is only skin deep
Why not explore the inner looks instead
Of being sheep!

Sheila Olivia Hogan

IN MY HEAD

In my head lives thoughts and wishes,
That whisper quietly and softly.
When the curtains close slowly,
I dream of things to come and go.
But when the devil casts a spell,
You dream of things you really
Don't want to know.
Around my head flies lots of dust.
Approaching my head are birds
Singing sweet quiet songs
But inside my head I think
No more.

Louise Simpkins (10)

BLACKTHORN AT WAINLODE

(by the Severn in Gloucestershire)

Above this wintered wood,
high-flying rackety rooks
speckle a blue-white sky.

Below steep banks,
the blind and winding Severn
threads through this shire land,

deaf to proud and distant bells
pealing their Sunday best.
Whispers of a season's awakening

are borne on a placid breeze.
Close by, thorns on twigs
remind me of another day, another hill,

and white petalled cups, too pure to touch,
impart a peace more set apart
than all our hallowed hopes.
Roger Pope

MUM

You gave me life,
You gave me love,
You always were the best,
The sweetest mum, the dearest wife,
It's time for you to rest.

I long to see your face again,
To sit you by my side,
And in this time of sorrow,
The Lord will be my guide.

Everybody loved you,
That was clear to see,
An extra special person,
Especially to me.
Beverley Turgoose

SAD LAD

I drive past him - walking slowly to school
Trudging as if in treacle
The daily walk
A long, lonely trek across bitter desert.
The only oasis - the last bell, 8 hours away.
What does he go home to?
I wonder in the warmth of my car
As I make the same journey
Over *very* different terrain.

He slouches into my classroom
Surly, bitter, sly.
Never asking questions
Except of my patience.
I am torn between my feelings
Of pity for his morning journey
And intolerance of his behaviour.
For, in this class of 20
I know he is still alone.

His flinch when reprimanded
Speaks of homely horrors.
The oasis of the last bell
Is merely a mirage
As he trudges back to home based horrors
Over his life's unchanging terrain.

Andrew Keen

FATE

Something is sending me wild.
It is deep down inside my mind.

My soul has been doubled.
I am in two minds.

One is of knowledge.
One is of pain.

I wonder which will shine through and give me my reign?
The one that is for my personal gain.

From time to time I feel they are both mine.
It is a shame I'm living on borrowed time.

I feel like a star preparing for the stage.
But then I feel it's time to turn over the page.

I am a man going in two different ways.
When will the light come to show me my reign?

Scott Kemp

LIFE/DEATH

People are too methodical.
This makes their mortal coil unwind and slow down
Until they begin to crumble.
Death is the crumbling of the mind
When this state is achieved, the person is either
Forgotten forever or treasured like a star that shoots
Across the sky.
So burn baby burn.

Austin Kemp

TEMPING

Are you the new temp reporting?
We've started a new line, it's for exporting.

We're pleased you managed to arrive
Here on time.
Your first tea break is at half past
Nine.

We won't interview you, I'll show you
The job, after which just ask, me
Name's Bob.

I can't believe it. Today's almost
At an end. Well if I'm asked, the
Answer's yes, I'm in the weekend.

Saturday's here, and I'm feeling queer,
They're expecting me in, I'll try it
See if I can work an hour,
I do feel so rough, where's me will power.

I knew it. In the end I just had
To go sick. Now I'd better get an
Appointment, with the doc, and quick.

So I've caught that bug, don't know
How I wasn't sick at the doc's,
I nearly was on that bright rug.

Oh damn, hope I didn't show this hole,
In me sock, know what, 1st time
I've seen that doc. Tomorrow morning
I can lay in till 8 o'clock.

Bill Denson

YE SONS OF THE ROCK

Come on Dumbarton ye sons of the rock
Let's give the big guns their annual shock
Rangers and Celtic were once filled with dread
When making a visit to fatal Boghead

Now it's silly Dumbarton we read in the mail
With a match well reported by big John McPhail
Just when were set for a run in the cup
The black and gold deliver another slip up

Come on Dumbarton may your funds never fail
Heaven forbid you a fate like the vale
Playing at Barrhead and Larkhall as well
While their rusty old hay sheds leaking like hell

Come on Dumbarton we'll sing evermore
Even though Bert Auld was pushed out the door
and the present Board of Directors have not a clue
Where to obtain another Sir Hugh

Come on Dumbarton make the crowd roar
As clever Martin Moohey opens the score
And when in the summer when promotion is won
Kit-man Dick Jackson can join in the fun

Stay there Dumbarton at your Miller Street home
Never sell out to some faceless gnome
Who'll bull-doze your fine meadow make your fans sore
And defile your green acres with a new super-store.

John O'Donnell

SHOPPING TRIALS

Can anyone explain to me
Why when you're in a shop
The goods that you most want most of all
Are always at the top

If you are of an average height
Or even if you are tall
It doesn't matter much to you
But me, I'm only small

When looking in the freezer chests
The goods you want to buy
Are always at the bottom
Can anyone say why

Would it alter life's great plan
If just once in a while
I could reach my purchases
Without stretching for a mile

Perhaps one day someone will make
A plastic bag that opens
So we won't have to struggle
Wetting fingers, stretching, blowing

I wonder when the shops are planned
Whether customers have a meaning
Do the people setting out the shops
Ever do the shopping?

S M Blanchard

OUR TOWN

Smoke belches from the chimneys
Is this a smokeless zone?
Surrounded by the noise and smells
Of industry pulsating wells
Of dust and fame
Traffic people bus and train
The glass works that are world renowned
Coal mine and chemical works are found
Knottingley that boasts the best
And offers work and place of rest
Canal and river run right through
Power stations are near too.
Boats and barges drift on by
Cooling towers that command the sky
I have looked but have not found
Any beauty here around.

Barbara Burdin

RELATIVES

Families should be there when we are in need
But so often they are too busy having their own families to protect and feed
In an ideal world we would all be brothers and sisters
But our paths are not always smooth and life often gives us blisters
Some families are large whilst others are small
With some members quite short and others so tall
Our relatives may make their fortune and fame
Whilst can barely manage to spell their own name
Yet things are often not as black and white as they seem
And there is always tomorrow and we can always dream.

Cherry Somers-Dowell

THE GATHERING

In an English castle garden fair
The poets breath bucolic air
Where bird and bough and flower and bee
Conjoin in perfect harmony.

Never was there brighter charm
As nature piped her Sunday psalm
Who's climax now, their evensong
When birds became a silent throng.

As bards, by inspiration's fire
Strummed songs of heroes on the lyre
And then, in purest rhyme so free
Recited tales of destiny.

Since those rolling years have passed
With Britain's shores so oft' harassed
The castle stands, in verdure fair
As disciples of the muse declare

That never was their blessed art so rich;
Indeed has reached a variety and pitch
Where flowing words in happy form serene
Still float across the ancient castle green.

Ted Herbert

AFTER

I cannot give the reasons,
I only sing the tunes.
The sadness of the seasons,
The madness of the moons.

Joseph Millson

SIMPLY LOVING YOU

The more I spend my life with you
The more it feels so right
The more I even think it through
I feel as high as a kite

Every day I see your pain
Every way I feel it too
Every year I see no shame
Just simply loving you

So this I say to you really means
My darling fair love Sue
For never in your wildest dreams
Will you find another so true

A fond farewell as I depart
With only a few words left to say
Our special love is in my heart
And more and more in every way.

Darren Finch

DON'T WEAR THAAT 'AT

Don't wear thaat 'at, I tol' 'er whilst yor crawlin' on the ground,
I'd settle for a cap, I said, when the shoot is goin' round.
Don't wear thaat 'at, I pleaded, it be fine enough it's true,
But I wouldn't wear thaat plumage while the shoot is passin' through.
Don't wear thaat 'at, I shouted, it'll bode no good, I said,
To be rustlin' through the undergrowth with feathers on yor 'ead.
'The shoot be damned,' she spluttered, 'Go away man, can't you see
That I'm searching for the nesting site of the Portugean bee.'
Later.
I dun mind this conversation laark, creatures 'ave their rights an' thaat,
But, as for thaat there city lass well . . . She should'na worn thaat 'at.

Susan Mullin

WELSHCAKE

If I was a curly-wurly
Would you rip me open fast?
Or carefully unwrap me
And chew me so I last?
If I was a CD
Would it be Carter or the Stuff?
If I was your body
Would you sit there in the buff?

If I was a condom
Would you make good use of me?
If I was a stripper
Would you pay to come and see?
If I was a Bic pen
Would you write a letter long?
If I was Big Ben
Would you be my big bong?
Or will you just be my Welshcake
Until the day we die
And then we can be quill-chums,
Right up there in the sky.

Elizabeth Quinn

SCHOOL'S OUT

The school bell rings at 3.15. I'm always there before,
Angelic little faces just inside the classroom door,
They tumble out with gappy grins, all rosy-cheeked and freckled,
With plimsoll-bags and reading books and jumpers all paint-speckled
They wave their notes importantly, that tell of bring and buys,
Verucas, missing uniforms and nits and beetle drives.
Proud owners clutch their models as they try to keep them whole,
Each one a masterpiece of yoghurt-pots and toilet roll
And all the upturned faces bright with loud and happy news,
Each knee a little scabbier, each shin can boast a bruise.
Still I await my six-year old, his classmates hurry past,
He swaggers out without a smile, invariably last.
He's always empty-handed, which deprives me of my due,
Not for us the Flora pots so carefully stuck with glue.
His socks are round his ankles and his laces are untied,
His jumper seems to be back-to-front, and he's left his coat inside.
My little cherub slouches up and lifts a languid brow,
My welcome smile melts to a sigh - I know what's coming now.
No spontaneous cuddle and no loving kiss for me,
A nod of recognition and 'I'm starving. What's for tea?'

Fran Somerville Reay

THE CYCLE OF LIFE

Conceived in loving union,
A new life has begun,
Silently the embryo in darkness,
Prepares to meet the sun.

The silent darkness is at an end,
Obscene and bold there's life,
To challenge the new born entity,
To battle against pain and strife.

Slowly with determination and learning,
He takes his place in life,
Doors open to the future,
Along winding paths of strife.

But the battle of life's not over,
When he takes to himself a wife,
New challenges then come before him,
Unfamiliar to him so far in life.

Troubles are many in parenthood,
When a new life has begun,
But as he gazes at the tiny infant,
He knows pride in his new born son.

But time the destroyer of us all,
Remorselessly speeds on its way,
He's reminded of the passing years,
As his golden hair turns grey.

He goes to meet his maker,
His duties on earth truly done,
He leaves them to his successor,
He leaves them to his son.

Reginald C Peach

SCHOOL DAYS

School is great, so they say
A happy time
So why did I cry and lie
And miss out on all the fun
To stay at home with mum.

Because it wasn't fun
Sitting on your own
Eating food I didn't like
Listening to boring teachers
Being thrown out in the cold.

No this isn't fun
I will cry and lie and stay at home with mum.

Bernadette Logan

BREATHLESS

Thanks so much for inviting me,
To contribute to your anthology,
Its inspiration I now desire,
To rejuvenate this ball of fire,
For literary art of word assembly,
As unpredictable as sport at Wembley.
Still untitled I soldier on,
Delighting you an hour gone,
Good luck wishes and salad veg.
Will leave me time to cut the hedge,
Again that sonnet has slipped away,
So please write back another day.

Jean Bannerjee

SUMMER DAYS

Lazy heat. All around.
Warm earth against my skin.
Drowsy feeling. Muffled sounds.
Lethargic dreams. To begin
Is not worth the effort;
To end is too hard. Just drift
In a soothing limbo. Caught
In time. Cease to exist.
Lose yourself - become as one
With the heat of the summer sun.

Pam Bailey

REMEMBERING

A cup of tea on Mother's Day
Brought up to me on a tray
The little things I remember are best
They come into my head when I have a rest

The tender touch of a child's kiss
It's nice to remember such things as this
When she brings me a bunch of flowers
When we sit around and talk for hours

I'm glad I had a daughter like the one I have
To have her makes me feel glad
And my son in law is like the son I never had.

I hope she has a daughter one day soon
I would be over the moon
She would get the pleasures money can't buy
The love of a child will make her cry.

A Carroll

GOD'S LITTLE MIRACLES

Children are precious presents
    from God up above

They're energetic and lively and
    give you lots of love

They make life so happy
    if you give them your heart
And after having children
    you won't ever want to be apart

Of course they can be naughty
    and mischievous too
But they'll always come back
    and say sorry to you

Always remember that children
    need love!

Teresa Crudgington

TO MY MOTHER

As you gaze upon this page
Do not look at ink black and paper white,
But see me at a younger age
When scared, or ill, late at night;
When only you could put things right.
With my triumphs, I wished to share;
I was proudest when you were there.
Do not think that as older I grow
A mother's love is of lesser value,
What I want is for you to know
That always I will think of you.

A M Barwani

31

TENDER HANDS

Such tender hands that hold us the moment we are born.
As we're carried to our mother, who's feeling tired and worn.
With out stretched arms receives us and takes us to her breast.
She smiles with pride at her babe as to her we're gently pressed.
Those two hands will guide us the path of life to go.
And down the years will teach us, all we need to know,
Lovingly she holds us when feeling ill or sad
Ever will she love us. Whilst we're behaving good or bad.
When we have troubles, we think too hard to bear.
She will whisper to you, your problems she will share
Ah! Mother's love cannot be measured not with rule or gauge.
She calms our spirits takes our hand so we are not afraid.
No-one cares just as much, though people may say they do
But you are truly mother's child, she'd give her all for you,
As the years take their toll, her hands grow gnarled and bent
Still there's love in that touch that's why a mother's sent.

K Wheatley

OH, PLEASE MAKE MY DAY

I got up this morning, found a hole in my sock
Then broke my shoelace as I glanced at the clock
As I heard a knock at the front door
I tipped the cornflakes all over the floor
I cut myself shaving, nothing went right
Shouting with pain, I gave the budgie a fright
I heard a letter drop onto the mat
While trying to get up I fell over the cat!
It was only the gas bill, to add to my woe
(I think I've lost my get up and go)
Now I feel so fed up and half dead
I think I'm going back to bed!

John McLeod

LULLABY FOR A SLOB

Go to sleep my yob, oh go to sleep,
Thank you for the company you keep!
As you're never working,
Misery is lurking.
This is what you've always been: A creep.

Take a look my moron, take a look!
You will never talk or read a book.
While you watch the telly,
On your dirty belly
I can see the rubbish that I cook . . .

If your slumber's light or if it's deep,
You are oh so nice when you're asleep!
When you're still and dreaming
I forget your screaming
And I am so happy I could weep.

Go to sleep, my brute, oh go to sleep,
Count the empty cans instead of sheep.
Mind you, all your thinking
Turns around your drinking,
You're just scruffy, lazy and you're cheap.

Never wake up, slob, and never rise,
Close your eyes forever, close your eyes.
When you're in your coffin
Then you'll stop your scoffing
And to me life will be paradise! . . .

S Fallon

GRANDMA'S ALBUM

Grandma's got an album.
She keeps it by her chair.
And unsuspecting visitors
Are forced to sit and stare
At old and faded photographs
Of days of long ago,
Of Christenings, weddings, birthday treats
And people they don't know.

Here's Fred and Pearl and Joe and Jane,
Old Bert and cousin Dee,
All dressed up in their Sunday best.
What a dreadful one of me!
And that's my old flame, Tommy Brown.
He was a handsome lad.
Looks better with is hat on, though,
Got ears just like his dad.

I'm sure that's cousin Mabel,
Sitting on that horse.
Oh yes, and Uncle Wilfred.
He's dead now, of course.
Aunt Beth and Uncle Arthur
At the mayor's inaugural lunch.
Sad their day was ruined
When his teeth fell in the punch.

Bright smiles wilt and shoulders sag,
Eyes begin to glaze,
They watch a lifetime's memories pass
Across each tissued page.
You've reached the end. That is a shame,
We were so thrilled to look.
I'm glad you liked it, Grandma says.
I'll get the other book!

Pat Hearn

DEATH OF A DAD

I had a dad, he left long ago.
What he's doing now I expect I know.
Drinking! More drinking! Even more drinking!
Pouring tears of me into his drink but never thinking.
His thoughts are in the gutter
And I don't matter.
Once he sat me on his knee
And played and joked and we were we.
I never see him now
A broken vow
A weak and twisted gut.
Driven on by his drunken strut.
I did nothing to offend
What can he do to amend?
He could stop his drink and give up his wife
Take me back into his life.
He won't; of that I'm sure,
For him with drink there is no cure.
So I'll go on as I've always done
Because away from me he always runs.
To where does he run?
With a gun to the sun.
He wants to shrivel and sigh
The end results to defy.
Fending the prey of the worldly wise
I'm sure he's hidden under a disguise
Somewhere surely is a tinge of kindness
It can't be all his stupid blindness
But I have a dad that's better than he
My mum helps out and accepts what comes to be
For my dad is God, the one above
As for my mum, she gives me lots of love.

Denise Shaw

LITTLE LUKE

I looked down at little Luke.
I thought just how perfectly formed he was.
Something so small yet so beautiful.
Our first child.
We had loved our baby from the moment
That we knew it had been conceived.
The months had sped by so quickly
And yet in some ways agonisingly slowly,
Hour after hour we had imagined it.
We had talked as though it was already born.
In every way a part of our world.
It had laid with us through each night
And walked with us through each day.
All our plans were made for the three of us.
Each day it had grown to completeness.
It had been protected until it was perfected.
Now here he was.
With a little cry he had arrived.
He had emerged into the outside world.
We had kept him to ourselves.
Now he was ours, but ours to share,
With the rest of his special family.
Aunts who had devotedly knitted for him.
Those who would ensure like us
That he would not lack love and attention.
What fun we would all have together.
Now we were truly a family.
Little Luke had made our happiness complete.
I asked him if he understood what he meant to us
His eyes were shut. It could wait until tomorrow!

John Christopher Cole

12TH BIRTHDAY

Such a dear sweet girl,
She's nearest to my heart,
That calamity of a Jane
Is always in a whirl,
Full of sparkle, whit and shine,
Loving and naughty but true,
All part of life's gift to you.

You've grown into a rose-bud,
Ready, just about to open
But small and neat and exquisite
Oh lord; that you have chosen,
Such perfectly formed images
That come in such small packages
Never to be broken.

So as you grow each day
From buddling into flower,
Think of all the fun we've had,
As life grows by the hour,
Always keep your chin held high.
The goals are for the future
The limits are the sky!

And as you precious flower
Bloom and flourish the whole summer through,
The day will come when you will be,
A strong adult mature and true.
This is the jewel of life you have,
Hold it whilst you can,
Cherish each precious moment,
Innocent and loving rose-bud
To break out into flower.

J A Hart

AND NOW THE PARTY'S OVER

I've been to a party, and I've had a ball,
With sandwiches and jelly,
With ice-cream cakes and all,
We danced upon the tables,
We even broke a chair,
We all began to laugh. We really didn't care,
But now I've got a tummy ache,
I think I'll go to bed,
Mum asks if I want a drink,
But I just shake my head,
I think I'll go to the toilet first,
I have to move quite quick,
Mum, she tries to cuddle me,
But that's when I am sick,
All down her dress, all on the floor.
It was even on the bathroom door,
My mum began to shout and scream,
'I think you ate too much ice-cream,'
Mum cleaned me up, and made me fresh,
And I went off to bed,
The thought of all the food I ate,
Was dancing in my head,
That's the last time I go to a party,
And eat such a lot,
I think I'll stick to lettuce leaves,
Then again maybe not!

Ellen Thompson

A NEW WORLD

Your head it turns to every sound
First hear and then you learn
Wide eyed you study all you see
Such freedom to discover
Small hands that touch most everything
You feel with fascination
For this is a new world you have found
My darling baby girl.

Jacqueline Harrison

RYAN

I don't know how I managed to fill my days before you came
along
I only know that they were filled with things that aren't
important now
Or how I lay in bed to nine or ten at weekends and still was
tired when Monday came
The most that I can hope for now are seven hours with only
two or three interruptions to take away the monsters in your
dreams
And when you fall and hurt yourself it's me you want to kiss
away the tears
I feel proud and strong to have the whole of your small body
clinging to my neck
I love to share the joy you feel on discovering some new skill
like hammering a plastic nail into a block or recognising
Grandpa in a photograph
I'm glad for now that I can protect you from the world
I wish it could always be like that.

R McKay

I WILL? WILL I?

No more planning now the morning has come,
Everything's ready that needs to be done.

The flowers are fresh, the dresses all pressed
It's six in the morning but no-one can rest.

Emotions excited but tinged with doubt
You'd better get ready now, ten voices shout.

Where's my tie? Where's my hat?
Oh no mum, don't make me wear that!

Where's the car? The photographer's here!
It all seemed so easy, now so unclear!

Where's the rings? I need a drink!
What hat do I wear the blue or the pink?

Everything's silent now, just me and dad
So very happy and a little bit sad.

As he holds my hand, we step into the car
The journey is short, but seems very far

All heads turn as I walk down the aisle,
As I look straight ahead and continue to smile

A few words spoken, two people now one
Formalities over, now starts the fun!

Yasmin Gere

WHEN NEEDED

When needed we will come to see
what help or service we can be.
How can we help, what can we do;
is our past experience of use to you?

We charge no fee, there is no cost;
only consultation time is lost.
Sometimes our knowledge is of use,
but mostly we're the last excuse.

A sounding board to echo others,
to confirm or deny what they have said,.
But then you follow what fancy takes you,
caring not, the conclusions read.

Distance doesn't heed a frequence,
but thoughts can travel unhindered miles.
The caring isn't changed by timespan,
but concentrated on whens and whiles.

No more emphasis on opportunity;
time and place are by design.
More store is put by every visit,
extra effort, - underlined.

Life is mainly what we make it,
but empty without those who care.
Friendships formed, may last and linger,
or die without a second spare.

Never mind, we have no worry,
pastures new will soon be seeded.
And while we wait for these to flourish,
we'll fill the gap again when needed.

Tricia Janes

RUSTIC MEMORIES

Each step we take,
In life's long road,
Each story that our grandfathers told,
Of winding streams,
And apple trees,
Of mistletoe and birds and bees,
The old mill,
For our daily bread,
The little chapel,
Where our prayers were said,
The smell of the oven,
Where grandmother baked,
The hay in the fields,
Which the men had raked,
The cockerel with its early morning call,
The Victoria plums,
Which began to fall,
September's here and fair of heart,
The old ironmonger,
With his rustic cart,
Now comes the winter,
With its heavy snow,
But soon the daffodils,
Will say hello.

Terry Devereux

THE FAIRY BABE

The little face appeared so frail
But then let out a howling wail.
Found just near a farmer's gate
As the clock was striking late.
Wrapped inside a worn out shawl,
Not old enough to even crawl.
A little face blue with cold
What a story to be told.
Uncle Billy brought her round
A baby girl that he had found
It really was a pitiful case
As we looked into her tiny face
She really was a lovely dream
With skin the colour of milky cream
Ebony curls upon her head
We laid her down on mamma's bed
And there, the moon-dust upon her hand
She must have come from fairyland
So we left the candles burning bright
Because fairies only came at night
We hid and waited behind the door
And we saw the fairies and many more
We were very quiet and did not tell
And now in our house the fairies dwell.

Josephine Aldred

43

THE THREE OLD MEN

One summer's day three ancient men sat on the village seat
awarming of their tired old bones all in that pleasant heat.
There came a passing journalist, who keen to earn his wage,
sought from them the secret how they reached their mighty age.
The first, all gnarled and wrinkled said, 'To me the way is plain
None but green food shall pass my lips, I'm vegetarian.
I'm hale and hearty, enjoy my days. 'Tis great to be alive.
You ask me what my age is sir? Why I be ninety five!'
The next old man, more ancient still though his eyes twinkled blue
cackled a while at just the thought some secret that he knew.
'Child, youth and man I've bided here and scorned both wine and
maid.
No drop of booze have I consumed, no woman have I laid.
I've been TT for all my days and also celibate.
You ask me what my age is sir? Why I be ninety eight!'
The last old man most ancient yet, gave out a wicked grin.
His eyes were sunken in his head and drool spilled down his chin.
'I sup roast beef and quaff red wine, a wench sat on each knee.
There's songs I've sung from morn till night while imbibing in all
three.
My life is one long picnic. One great feast of fun.
You ask my age sir? 'Tis the truth. Why I be twenty one!'

Bob Everett

TONI THE MIMIC

I remember Toni, when she was only three.
Said to me in the kitchen
'I want a cup of tea.'
'What do you say' said I
Feeling a wee bit crankie,
She looked at me, with a glint in here eye
'I want a cup o' tea Frankie!'

Now she wants a biscuit and another
And another
Getting fed up with this I said
'You'll have to ask your mother.'

Toni, oh Toni, are you no nearly foo,
She crunched and munched and swallowed
And said 'Oh aye the noo.'

By here wee Toni, you don't half like
The freebies
She laughed and giggled, 'Oh pappa' she
Said 'You give me the heebie jeebies.'

Frank Sutherland Johnson

SMOKERS

Smokers smoke like smoky chimney
pots filling their lungs with toxic
smoke which will choke them,
but do they stop no they
can't as they're playing a deadly
game that they can't ever
win but only lose their life
one day.

Michael Spittles

MY DREAM

Eileen's got Alex the toy boy,
Her granddaughter's got sugar daddy John
And I'm alone by the river
With the moon just looking on

My blanket's on the ground
My back against a tree
Then suddenly a movement
Not far away from me

My heart starts beating very fast
What ever can it be?
It's even coming closer
I might just manage to see

If I stand on tip toe
As quietly as can be
A knight in shining armour
Might be looking just for me

But then the thing I saw
Was not a shining knight
It was the morning sun
Shining through my window
With all my dreaming done

The birds were trilling in the trees
The flowers fresh with dew
Then it will be Saturday
To share my dream with you.

Audrey Cooper

JANUARY SALES

Slimming in January - Christmas ahead.
Presents and plum duff our waists do spread
Turkey and cranberry, sausage and chips
All put the inches on our ample hips.

Forward to '95 aim for the least
Swimming and dieting - give us no feast
Come on you healthy ones cut out the toast
Think of the outline that you love the most.

Ladies and gentlemen look to your style
Sales clothes are ace if they bring you a smile
Jeans will fit better and smarter by far
If inches are shed then you'll soon be the star.

Gog

JADE'S FIRST STEPS

My cousin named Jade took her first steps today
It took a lot of determination I must say
She took those steps with such delight
Her face beamed like the sun so bright
She got her balance and took one step
And with open arms she was met
A great applause and a big hug too
She received as walking to her was something new
Everyone was so proud of Jade
Which is why Jade's day was made.

Louise Thomson

BEHIND THE MASQUERADE

What lies behind the masquerade
of a man who plays the clown,
does he have some pain to hide
from a soul that's broken down.

Upon the white mask of paint
a single teardrop is placed,
is this a constant reminder
of the loneliness so often faced.

Around the mouth in deepest red
an exaggerated grin he'll portray,
the laughter lines are etched there
but the eyes show his dismay.

The artistry is then completed
with baggy clothes and big red nose,
what lies behind the masquerade
of the clown in the circus shows?

Sue Jackson

NOVEMBER

No butterflies,
No bees.
No playing,
No Easter,
No trees.
No ants,
No fresh seas.
No Christmas,
November.

Jevon Hendrix Davies (8)

MY VEGETARIAN DREAM

Cabbages, cabbages are everywhere.
In every room, on every stair,
Cabbages, cabbages all down the road.
I even saw one, under a toad!
Thirty-one lay on my bed,
And thirty-two inside my head.
So out I plucked them from my ear,
And laid them down upon the stair.
I went downstairs to make some tea.
Then lifted the pot, but there to see,
Just in the corner, and blocking the spout,
Was a tiny red carrot, and one brussel sprout.
I then lifted my eyes, and looked all around.
But no carrots or cabbages were to be found.
I'd been chopping carrots and slicing some greens,
Just last night, after ironing my jeans.
I then looked all around and felt very glad,
As I realised it was a dream I had had!

C Flowers

SCORE

The crowd jostled and rushed to the front
hot and sweaty bodies push, groan and grunt
the gates laid open for the swelling crowd
but each one dead all covered in a shroud
cocooned in a sleeve held tight in a sea
but each one dead no swimmers to be
hearts pounding fast, sweat flowing free
two lovers entwined in love so cosy
the crowd stop pushing the end of a siege
but not one came forward to plant a seed
the other side didn't reply except in will
so at the end of the day the score was one-nil.

Robert Lawrence-Jones

49

IT'S NOT FOR ME

I'm glad I'm not Prime Minister of Britain, not a job that is from heaven sent.
Main part of work is done in front of public, with people questioning your each intent.
On your feet for hours to get a bill passed, when it's done you rush on home for tea,
No sooner you've begun upon wife's cooking, phone call says you're needed hurriedly.
Arabs and Israelis have a difference, solve it or could lead to your downfall.
Hours later, having done all that is needed, you know no praise for it you'll get at all.
From number Ten you go next to the Palace, it's necessary you talk with the Queen.
About another trip she will be making, thankfully she soon grasps what you mean.
Cabinet awaits so you must brief them, up to date with country's main affair.
Go to House of Commons to tell members, then hold big discussion on it there.
Opposition argues very strongly, they could do a better job than you.
Ministers spring hotly to defend you, saying our Prime Minister's true blue.
Just to be a minister would also, fail to be a job that heaven sent,
Even less so is to be the Premier, with task of leading Britain's government.

Barbara Goode

POLITICS - NOT FOR ME

Vote for me
Vote for me
I'll do this
I'll do that
If only you will vote for me
That is what we hear for weeks
So when it is over it is such a relief

Labour, conservative and liberals too
All promising what they will do
Others standing for different things
Saying what they will do if they win

Red, blue and green
All colours to be seen

Our TV shows are disturbed
The politicians really have got a nerve
For me voting times are a bore
With people canvassing at the door

All the papers saying every day
Is it will soon be voting day
And when we go to pick up our post
There's leaflets saying don't forget to vote

But who's ever won or lost
I couldn't give a toss
As politics don't interest me

For they are all the same as far as I can see
Vote for me
Vote for me
I'll do this
I'll do that
If only you will vote for me.

Eileen Kyte

51

CLAIR DE LUNE

In the still of the night, after the long day is through . . .
When I'm alone and dreaming, my thoughts and longing for you return
over and over again . . .
Memories of the past and those happy days when you came into my life
and it seemed . . .
That my world became a wonderland, when into my arms you stepped
out of a dream . . .

From the rays of the moonlight when you first appeared . . . Your smile,
the blue of your eyes . . .
The sparkle of moonbeams aglow in your hair . . .
It was love at first sight, a love that will never fade, and will always
and forever be there . . .

You know darling, you were, and always will be, deep in the heart of me . .
.
So deep in my heart, you're really a part of me . . .
Kneeling, under a heavenly ceiling, I say a prayer to the heavens above . . .
And appealing, to bring back, to me my love . . .

With you it would have been happiness and the rekindling of that special
flame . . .
In my dreams, again and again, it seems I hear you call my name . . .
My day begins and ends with thoughts of you, and my whispering
softly your name to . . .
It's hidden in this phrase with words endearing and embracing all that is
you . . .

They are simply . . . beloved . . . embraceable . . . thrilling . . .
true love . . . yearning . . . All life through . . .

Do I awake from a romantic past, for there you stood, the same as I
dreamed you would . . .
For you have come back to me . . . My first love at last . . .

Douglas Ralph Bisset

HEROES

Our parents sacrifice everything for us,
How do we thank them?
We kick up a fuss.
As a child we dream of what we want,
Or what we want to be,
And if we don't get it who gets the blame,
It's the one who's closest to me.
Do they complain or go to their room,
Or sit at the dinner table full of gloom,
No they stick it out, and it isn't until
We get older until we finally get a clout.
They put up with tantrums and
Slamming of doors,
And when they've finally had enough
Everyone dives for the floor.
But they are heroes to put up with it all,
Although many would say that we
Have to put up with more!
But overall my hero would have to be,
Someone who is very close to me.
My hero doesn't have a cape or X-ray vision
And that's because she doesn't need them.
My hero saves people, but in another way,
She saves souls, and saves the day.
My hero is always there for me,
She taught me my a-b-c.
She was there for me when I fell from a tree,
And was there when I lost my two front teeth.
I know that my hero is always there for me,
No matter what I do!

Elisha Ariss

MY TOY BOX

As I was searching in my toy box
I came across *one* of Dad's blue socks.
Now I know that it doesn't live in there
but if I can find the other one I'll have a pair.

Next I found *two* broken drumsticks,
the ones that Mummy refused to fix.
She said, 'Why, when you've got all these lovely toys,
do you want the ones that make the most noise?'

Further and further I went down
and discovered *three* things that belong to my clown.
His hat, bow-tie, and bright red nose,
I wonder if Clowny Man has been looking for those?

I continued to look amongst the games
and found *four* dolls without any names.
Now dolls without names, that just won't do
so I'll call them Bill and June and Pete and Sue.

Look! There's *five* books that I haven't read.
Tonight I'll take them all to bed
and when Mum and Dad think I'm asleep
I'll open the books and have a peep.

All of these things I didn't know were there,
in my toy box under the stairs.
Six building bricks, all different sizes.
Perhaps there'll be even more surprises.

Seven coloured pencils and a colouring book.
Eight pots and pans in which to cook.
Pretty glass marbles, counting there's *nine*.
Ten racing cars, all of them mine.

All of my treasures are now on the floor,
but I've forgotten what I was looking for.
So I'll put the toys back in their box,
all except for Dad's blue sock!
David Metters

NOTHING

What did we do at school today?
We didn't do nothing.
It's true Miss Pierce
Told us about taking away -
Taking away leads to nothing!
PC Plod gave a talk about riding your bike,
I ain't got a bike, all I can do is walk -
So that was nothing!
And Miss Andrews showed us
Some pictures about making babies -
(Clive saw an old poster on which was written
You gotta keep babies out of Britain)
And I said, 'Yes, all ours makes is a noise and a mess;'
It's worse than nothing!
At break we played kiss chase
And I got caught by Darren Wilkes:
I couldn't keep his ugly mug away from my face -
Ugh, he's worse than nothing!
And, when it was time to go home
John said, 'Eyes together and hands closed:'
I giggled, and the Head, who was passing by
Said, 'Come to my study, Amanda.'
So I'll get a good talking to,
But that'll be nothing!

L V S Taylor

SONNET OF A SITE AGENT

My life in Civil Engineering is quite tough,
We work long hours in mud and rain,
Our Irish labour force is fairly rough,
More noted for its brawn than for its brain.
The programme for the job is always tight,
The weather must not make completion late,
The work must all be finished on the site,
By the client's all-important contract date.
But as I watch construction work progress
Because I've organised it reasonably well,
I know a feeling almost of elation.
My salary is probably much less
Then I could earn indoors, but hell!
I'm happy in my chosen occupation.

Bob Bridgman

DAVID'S DELIGHT

Late one evening on Christmas Eve,
I heard a noise on the rooftop eaves,
Through the window I peeped outside,
But no-one was there; to my surprise
I again heard the noise downstairs below,
So off I crept, on tip-toe.
Halfway down I held my breath,
Cold and shivery - half undressed!
I reached the door and entered in,
And wished, oh, please let it be him!
I switched on the light and turned to see
He was there and standing by the tree,
'Ho, Ho!' Merry Christmas, David,' he said with cheer,
And with a sparkling flash, he disappeared!

David William Lowe

56

ONE AUGUST NIGHT

I coughed then cursed myself, for having made a noise
That lapse in concentration, wasn't very wise
The monster surely heard it, so much for my guile
His evil face would now, be twisted in a smile

My watch said 3am, the forest was pitch black
I gripped my weapon tightly, soon he will attack
Standing motionless 'neath that tree had turned my feet to ice
Perhaps I should have listened, to old *Hooks'* advice
'Stay away' *Hooks* had growled, 'from the unseen one's home
Else he might be ripping, the flesh from off your bone'

But old *Hooks* had forgotten, one important factor
The monster *had* been seen, by that man called Baxter

Almost two years ago, young Baxter (mushroom picking)
Saw a sight he later called, 'Sad and sickening'

A mother and three offspring, that bright August morning
Exploring this same forest, then without warning
The huge monster appeared, ignoring Baxter's roars
Seized the mother's youngest, in its massive jaws.

That poor little youngster, was never seen again
And subsequent searchings, have all been in vain.

That mother can't be traced, Baxter's emigrated
The public lost all interest, 'cept for me, I waited
Waited for two long years, 'til the time was right
At last the waiting's over, tonight will be the night.

Over there, by the swamp, rising from the ground
Two angry looking eyes, a low growling sound . . .
       'That tent is freezing cold, I must be off my head
       Married to a fisherman. That maggot must be dead.
       The float ain't moved for hours, bet that pike's a kip
       All this 'cos of a duckling . . . I'm sure that you have flipped.'

Billy Brindle

MARKS AND SPENCER

There's a certain company
   held in the highest esteem,
Its rise to fame,
   started as a dream.
From penny bazaar,
   in a market in Leeds,
To a top retail store
   in London, indeed.
Marks and Spencer soon came to be,
A name synonymous,
With value and quality.
Conscientious employees, dedicated and loyal,
They belonged to the *Firm*
   just like the royals.
So, the honours go to one and all,
From their humble beginnings
   on that market stall.
To a company that's proven,
   beyond any doubt,
That customer care,
   is what it's all about.

Polly Cox

MY LOVE

Fleeting smile gentle touch words
Soft spoken mean so much
A quiet haven from daily care
to find at last a life to share
A love, that binds two souls as one
yet leaves the spirit free to run
To grow in stature bound yet free
this is the measure of your love for me.

Edna Sarsfield

BORN IN THE COUNTRY

I was born in the country,
     began work at fifteen,
Life took on a new vision,
     I had a new dream,
To work hard was expected,
     the hours were long,
No time to laugh or sing a song,

We loved the animals
     dogs, pigs and cows,
Their life was part of this earth of ours,
Now what has happened as we look around
     can we not hear a different sound,
My vision is blurred I no longer dream,

Man has destroyed this happy scene,
Trees are cut down, fields and valleys have gone
     and yes my friends there is a bomb,
Computers and tellies are here to stay
     we don't send our children out to play,
They sit indoors and watch the box,
     consider please where is Mr Fox,
Open your eyes, your mouth and your heart,
     let's preserve creation please play our part,
As soon as you recognise what's going on,
     You will say to *God*,
Thy will be done.

Patricia Bray

BORN AND BRED IN THE POTTS

Ah conner say that ar'm Aryish,
or Welsh, that'l never dow.
Ah conner say that ar'm Scottish,
or ar'l get in a rate ouwd stew.
Ah conner say that ar'm foreign,
tho' foreigners, wave got lots.
But one thing ah con see, withite any fear,
Ar'm born and bred in the potts.

A wudner wish ta bay else weer
fer the potts is me pride and joy,
An alweese as been since me dad
sent me work in um as a boy.
Two pinde a wic an seven an six
that's the lot fer me tac oom pay.
Ah didner grumble neow not then
fer it wanner too bad yer say.

Fer some were scarce tacin wom two quid,
But may, ah wus goowing fer.
Ah dramed a me avin me ouwn ice,
ah wanted call nowbody, sir.
So ah worked lark a trooper dee in an dee ite,
While me mam cut me sandwich a chayse.
Ah wanner un appy, but ah wanteed more
Ah wus just a mowd runner them deys.

Then ah met Iris on same pot bank,
She wus a paintress, high class.
Ah cudner tac me eyes off er
when at dinner tarms weeyed pass.
Er eyes erd fetch ducks off the wayter
an mine didner do too bad.
So ta cut a long story short, ar ad a word with er dad.

Then ah asked fer promotion ta bring up me pay,
A thowt ah wus due fer a raise.
Thee put me at mowd making, that wus the tops.
So Iris an may were quaite playsed.
Then came the dee on me wedding, and from now on ard pull all the shotts
ah adner done too bad seeying, ard started rate dine in the potts.

Dorothy M Collier

LEO

This old guy roams around our town
Shabby clothes and shoes worn down
Big, long beard and dirty face
Hear people say, 'Oh what a disgrace'
Sleeping on the street at night
He does no harm and he's alright
Leo is his name you know
This old man he takes life slow
Smoking fag butts from the ground
Checking bins but nothing found
He came into the cafe one day
A cup of tea he had money to pay
As he sat down with shaking hands
And began to sip his tea
A lad came up and said to me
'Why does he come here, why don't he leave?'
His money's good as you have seen
It's not for me to make a scene
Just leave him alone and let him be
He'll never say nowt to you or me.

Ted

(TELEPHONISTS) SHARP SPEAKING STRAIGHT TO THE POINT

The seeds are sown
The grass has grown
I've done well to hone
My thoughts are now rounder than stone

I'm connected to the philosophical phone
And mastered the tailored tenacious tone
So adversaries groan in gullibility
They lack the insight to see
They just can't psyche out me
As I've controlled to free my metered mentality

Years of frustration of convoluted conversation
Have stood me in good stead
As I've got to grips with the skills
Of surmounting heavy hills
And now temperate talking gives me tasty and telling thrills
Especially when I win the word war of the wills.

Tay Collicutt

SCRAMBLED PROGRAMS

You speak, you speak, you dare to speak before
I put the program in
You answer, you answer, the wrong answer; I did
not put those instructions in
Turn off the computer; let's start again - check
the book
This is the way the program goes in

The right answer is displayed
Now, no reason to be dismayed
Good! Good!
Leave the machine on.

Tricia Spring-Benyon

CHRISTMAS

Collecting my thoughts having been in a trance,
   After working with another 'twas . . . but sweet, perchance.
We were rostered together on Christmas Day,
   Looked forward to seeing her . . . so much to say.

Felt somewhat uneasy! For the presents I'd bound -
   A rebuff for my gesture . . . a darkened cloud?
In suppressing my feelings of her to me
   Depressions were heightened in soliloquy.

Given thoughts were unfounded, the occurrence seen,
   A lesson was learned of equanimity.
A joyous occasion . . . I will remember always,
   Scribed on my heart and there it will stay.
For the gift that was given meant so much to me.
   Response to such feelings . . . are of equanimity?

Aled Morris

LATE FOR SCHOOL

Wake up, wake up, you're gonna be late
We'll never get there at this rate,
Up out of bed, pull up your sock
Look at the time, it's eight o'clock
Come on, come on quick get dressed
Get a move on, your hair's all messed
Quick, quick, get in the car
Because we've got to go very far
We just made it to the school gate
And it's just turned half past eight.

Jenny Myers (13)

WITCH'S CAKE

In the cauldron boil and bake
ingredients for the witch's cake
to start . . .
In goes the sock of a football team's coach
helped along by a smelly cockroach
Some dustballs from old witch's broom
For good healthy food I have no room!
A big, hairy wart from witch's nose
A rat's tail and its toes
boil and bake
boil and bake
The noisy tail of a rattle snake
Try the witch's cake, you'll see
it's as tasty as can be
with ingredients recommended by me!

Stephanie Dawson

UNTITLED

Ah! Blackbird, call up the sun,
Doubts fade, thy note has won
A place in heaven where life began.
Ah! Blackbird, herald the dawn,
Sign-post night's end
Here hope is reborn.
Ah! Blackbird, sing me your song,
Await me in heaven
I'll follow the throng.

Leonard Whitehead

PSALM 23 FOR BUSY PEOPLE

The Lord is my pace-setter, I shall not rush
He makes me stop and rest for quiet intervals.
He provides me with images of stillness
Which restore my serenity.
He leads me in the ways of efficiency,
Through calmness of mind; and his guidance is peace.
Even though I have a great many things to accomplish each day
I will not fret, for his presence is here.
His timelessness, his all-importance will keep me in balance.
He prepares refreshment and renewal
In the midst of activity.
By anointing my mind with the oils of tranquillity,
My cup of joyous energy overflows.
Surely harmony and effectiveness
Shall be the fruits of my hours,
For I will walk in the pace of my Lord
And dwell in his house forever.

Toki Miyashina

UNDER MY BED

There are lots of dolls
And coloured balls
There are smelly socks
And building blocks
There are four toys
That don't make a noise
Some packing bags
And lots of rags
A picture of me
And splash of tea
Lots of sweet papers
And an old pair of slippers.

Nicola Stewart (9)

JOBBING GARDENER

Digging, raking, planting, sowing,
Edging borders, sweeping, mowing.
Taking cuttings, budding roses,
Making wreaths and young brides' posies.
Potting plants all neat in rows,
Laying flags for patios.
Larch-lap fence to be erected,
Restoring gardens long neglected.
Days of sunshine, wind and showers,
Hanging baskets filled with flowers.
Pruning roses, trees and shrubs,
Bedding plants for garden tubs.
Securing plants with stake and tie,
Each spring the lawns to scarify.
Trying to control those slugs,
Aphids, wireworms, mealy bugs.
Summer, autumn, winter, spring
Each season different tasks they bring.
Rebuilding walls, repairing gates,
Decorating floats for village fetes.
A chat, a smile, a cup of tea,
My customers fuss over me,
For they perceive my work and toil,
Brings beauty springing from the soil.
The diversity of plants amazing,
Oh dear, your greenhouse needs reglazing!
Is gardening an occupation
Or is it part of life's creation?
Along life's way I gently plod,
Happy to work alongside God.

David A Garside

MY FRIEND JESSIE

Her name was Jessie. She came every Tuesday
to our Lunch Club, and had a good feed.
She lived in a one-roomed flat down by the river
and her life was a sad one, a sad one indeed.

She was widowed, and then her young son had been drowned.
She said to me, 'Happiness I can't regain.
My loved ones are gone.' It was then that she took
to the bottle, trying to blot out her pain.

Every Wednesday afternoon I went to see her.
But one hot Wednesday I fell asleep.
On the couch. And I did not wake up again
'til the family came home. Sleep was so deep.

'I'll let Jessie know' I thought in a panic.
Wrote a letter and posted it over the way.
And then I went home feeling very much better,
thinking she'd get my letter next day.

Alas! I did not dream of what I would face.
For a policeman was waiting. Said Jessie had died.
Not that day but yesterday. I wasn't with her.
At home I was fast asleep. I sat and cried.

I was asked to identify poor Jessie's body.
In the mortuary a sheet was pulled gently away.
There Jessie lay, not yet dressed for her burial
while I was home sleeping upon her last day.

She was buried, and only three people were there.
I laid my red roses down by the grave-side,
and as I walked home I thought 'Oh my dear Jessie,
how I wish I'd been holding you close when you died.'

Marjorie Mitchell

UNTITLED

Loosely lipped, I view the scene
Mind wandering, occasional dream
Of things to be, and times past
When conquering thoughts, stilted; last
For a moment, we imagined we were there
Eyes fixed, non plussed, vacant stare.
The warmth of the sun, the smell of the air
Walking barefoot in blue seas, I wake. Sand in my hair!
These split second meanders I have now and then
Seems just like reality and better often.
The intermissions of life, I love more and more
Reality scolds and chafes a bad sore
We all try to heal, but no-one has the answer
Of life is too short, our genes. Faded, nice pair.
The answer you'll not find in an avenue of time
Between the trees you might glimpse the illusion . . . mine.

Peter Sharpe

AN EVERGREEN TREE

Spiky tinsel,
Spiky tree,
          the lights are bright and hot.
There are drums on the Christmas tree,
          and an Angel on the top.
A star twinkling on the Christmas tree,
          Presents at the bottom of the tree,
          Baubles hanging,
          they are silver, and red,
          A horse, noisy bells,
          a glittering Angel,
And Father Christmas and a snowflake.

Stephanie Joseph (4)

TIMES REMEMBERED WHEN YOUNG

How lovely were the fields,
When I was young.
There would I stand and gaze,
Upon the golden buttercups
Gleaming in the noon-day sun.
Patient cows stand idly by,
With flick of ear and swishing tail
Against tormenting fly.

How lovely were the lanes
In those early days.
With mossy banks so green
Tall trees arching overhead
Shielding us from hot sun's rays.
Wild flowers peeping through the grass
Enticing bee and butterfly
To greet us as we pass.

And lovely were the village ponds
There we used to stand,
Searching for the tadpoles
Wriggling in and out the reeds,
Some we caught by hand,
But always set them free again,
For frogs one day they'll be,
And hop around on land.

Margaret Z Tunnell

THE TWENTY-FIRST CENTURY

The twenty-first century always meant to me
A space-age of rockets and flying saucers
Forbidden planets and alien life forms
Of a nice clean planet for us to live
No need to work just free time
A quality life for us all to enjoy
We'd have flying cars so we could fly
Right up into the sky so high
In the mid nineties it became so clear
That none of these things would yet appear
For it was like waking up
From a dream of futures yet to come
Back in the real world nothing much changes
Life still goes on by day to day from year to year
Time flies by us without a fuss
The twenty-first century almost upon us
And still I dream of things to come
The twenty-second century that's the one
For new technology and peace on earth
But not for me for I'll be through
And never to see my dreams come true.

David Allen

70

MY GARDEN

I have a garden of my own,
And in it are some seeds I've sown.
Like cornflowers, pansies, pinks and stocks
Forget-me-nots and hollyhocks.

For weeks and weeks I've paid attention
To my garden, not to mention,
All the watering required,
And so I'm feeling rather tired!

I think how lovely it will be
When all my flowers are there to see.
With colours yellow, pink and blue;
The air will all be scented too.

Ah, now at last my plants have grown.
But nowhere are the ones I've sown!
Instead the garden's full of thistles
Daisies, clover, stinging nettles.

But what is this before my eyes?
The sky is full of butterflies!
They flutter down, they love my weeds,
And so do all the birds and bees.

With butterflies red, white and blue,
With buzzing bees and songbirds too,
I sit and gaze all summer long.
Can next year all my seeds go wrong?

Jean Streader

NONSENSE! OR IS IT?

A crowd of chairs, sat round the dining table,
The drinking glass, was having too much coke,
The curtains drew together, wouldn't let another see;
And a cigarette went missing in the smoke.

The video recorded the commotion
To the table - undercover of a cloth.
'Twas a lighter did the deed, made it disappear at speed
So a pen wrote out a cheque to hide the loss.

The video recorded the commotion,
And a pencil, put the picture in the frame;
Seems that there must be a catch, for I'm told that it's no match
And the matches shouted 'We were not to blame!'

A crowd of chairs, sat round the dining table,
The drinking glass was having too much coke;
The curtains drew . . . together, wouldn't let another see;
And a cigarette went missing in the smoke.

Paul Imbriani

FAMILY

When one has family all around
What more can a mum ask.
To keep that love so strongly bound
It should be no great task.
God bless my family one and all
They're all so great to me
I want them to walk straight and tall
For all the world to see.

Iris E Siddons

SCENERY

White clouds; blue and turquoise sky. Brown sea. Black ships.
Red and orange metal bridge - falling down on the black ships.
Law in the bottom left corner. White, tall, blocks for buildings;
stand in front of the
blackened and burnt out buildings. Everything becomes grey
in the background.

Green fields. Broken down and ruined grey wall. Brown wood tree.
Green fields. Black broken down and ruined church or cathedral.
Blue sky. Red clouds. Close to home.

Red fields. Broken down and ruined grey wall. Blue wood tree.
Red and pink fields. Black broken down and ruined church or cathedral.
Yellow sky. Orange clouds. Close to now.

Blue fields. Broken down and ruined wall. Red wood tree.
Blue shaded fields. Black broken down and ruined church or cathedral.
Purple sky. Red clouds. View from my window.

Andrew Poots

THE PICTURE

I fell into a picture once
It was so pretty there
A little stream, a waterfall
And flowers everywhere
Trees of green blew back and forth
And a warm wind did blow
The sun shone bright, a bluebird took flight
And my life was all aglow
A little white cottage lay back in the distance
Of the trees but as I blinked reality struck
The picture was only in my dreams.

Stephanie Brown

73

A COLD

Nose dripping like a waterfall
Brow damp with dry mould
Throat aflame cough choke
Muscle bone in retreat
Temperature up spirits down
Mental state a total frown
Short in temper full in pride.

Paracetamol, aspirin, Lemsip
Traditional cures for various nose drips
None work none can
Only body's time helps
No cure for something unknown
Professors of medicine seek a cure
No closer than a thousand years ago.

Do you need a cold
Or does a cold need you?

Derek Young

FIRST IMPRESSION

Intent on their conversation
Two young women bend toward each other
Softly folded into the creased light
Of their table by the dark wall
Their clothes as if fitted
Loosely about their whispers
To suggest inflection, innuendo
By each gesture of silence and laughter
Of two friends studied by a stranger

Johnjoseph Pajor

UNTITLED

Why not start to play indoor bowls
It's a lovely hobby for young and old.
Meeting new people making new friends
Learning the way your forehand bends.

Play in the leagues week after week
The dark evenings you find, pass in a tweak.
Now my ambition is to play for the club
I think I have now caught the bug.

This weekend I have been selected
An honour which was so unexpected.
Good heavens above I've got no whites
Down to the shop to put things right.

Listening eagerly to the captain's address
The etiquette rules are rigidly stressed.
No drinks on green, of smoking there's none
And what about running, it's *strictly* non! Non!

Next week I've been told the National Fours
Is taking place within our local doors.
I've been advised to go as a spectator
To watch and learn from better partakers.

But what I found to my surprise
That the captain's address from verse five.
No longer applies to National Players
As they hare up and down like Grand National chasers.

Etiquette to others on either side *forgot*
Shouting and shaking hands after every shot.
Is this the same game that I've been taught
It's too late to stop now, all the equipment I've bought.

J Harrison

POOR JANIE

Janie was blind and getting old
Then she got lost out in the cold
She was also deaf, she wandered far
Passed by many driving a car
Passed by people walking by
No-one heard her silent cry
Hungry now feet red raw
Would no-one open a friendly door
I hope when I get frail and old
I'm not left forgotten in the cold
Selfish people with hearts of steel
Eyes that turn away, can't they feel
Cold icy roads and freezing fog
It shouldn't happen to a dog
But it did to Janie blind and old
There was no warm welcome to the fold
Those who passed her, had turned away
Your day of reckoning will come one day
And if you're lost in the snow and fog
Remember poor Janie a lost blind dog.

Connie Deane

MY VEGETARIAN DREAM

Cabbages, cabbages are everywhere,
In every room on every stair.
Cabbages, cabbages are down the road
I even saw one under a toad.
Thirty-one lay on my bed,
And thirty-two inside my head.
So out I plucked them from my ear,
And laid them down upon the stair.
I went downstairs to make some tea,
They lifted the pot, but there to see,
Just in the corner and blocking the spout,
Was a tiny red carrot and one brussel sprout.
My eyes then slowly opened
I looked all around,
But no carrots or cabbages were to be found.
I'd been chopping carrots and slicing some greens,
Just last night after ironing my jeans.
I looked all around and felt very glad,
As I realised it was just a dream!

C Flowers

SNOWDROPS

I see your white heads pushing high,
Pushing upwards to the sky,
Up through the green grass,
Up from the dark at last.
You know the winter is here,
And it's next month you should appear,
You should come in February,
When it's crisp and clear,
But you pushed so hard,
And January you appear,
You sweet little flower,
Your white head's nodding
Sends my heart bobbing,
And fills me with cheer
So snowdrop keep coming,
Year after year.

Shirley Rowland

THE NAMING OF RUTH

We named Ruth today.
We put her in the water.
We sprinkled her with champagne.
Five of us then sat on her,
Then rowed her away.

For Ruth is a sleek rowing boat, built for speed.
As she skims across the water,
Sleek like a bird.
The sun shone off her bow,
Way across the water.
Rowed with power, muscle and sinew.
Fast across the water, Ruth our new rowing boat.

P J Altoft

A GLIMPSE OF HELL

I watched apart,
I stood in fear,
Too torn apart,
To shed a tear.

For all the tears,
That heaven shed,
Could not wash,
That moment's dread.

To leave my soul,
Unburdened, new,
I stood surveyed,
All hell my view.

And in my soul,
A tempest wild,
The day I almost,
Lost my child.

Elizabeth Whitehead

KEEPING BUSY

I've plenty of time since I lost my man
So I keep as busy as I can
I'm now into sewing, poetry too,
Urged on by the letters I've had from you.
Knitting, tapestry, all these things
The sense of achievement this all brings
I've created some pictures, they hang on my wall
And they are often seen, and admired by all
Cushion covers, table cloths too
All been embroidered by you know who
So if you are alone, bored or upset
Start on a hobby, contentment you'll get.

Alice Stapleton

79

YOUR FIRST HOUSE

Your house is now ready -
   exciting and bright;
You'll both be so proud
   as you lock up each night.
There's a hundred and one things
   that you're going to do -
The housework - the garden -
   and that's only two!
Consider the decor - the lighting -
   and heat.
And bills and demands
   that you'll both have to meet.
But now - most important -
   togetherness first.
The promises made must be
   nurtured and nursed.
Just treasure each other as
   husband and wife
This is the first day of the
   rest of your life!

R Mayor

SADIE

A little stranger walked in on our family
Begraggled, afraid, lonely and hungry,
She was fed, she was warmed, she was happy,
Her fur coat began to glisten amber eyes bright.

She made our hearts rejoice with her funny little way
Sometimes she is aloof and doesn't want to play.
She's grown contented, happy and strong
And is served gourmet meals all along.

She has a friend called Blackie,
Who calls around each day
He comes to share a meal with her
No wonder one might say.

She's given our hearts much gladness
It's very plain to see
The beautiful cat with the amber eyes
Adopted us that special day.

Doris Kitching

LOVE'S TOO DEMANDING

Love's too demanding it expects
Total commitment and respect.
We cannot love each human being,
Those close to us give life more meaning.

We can be-friend and show concern
For other people, also learn
Through others when they do good turns.

Love too most means a big cuddle.
To embrace all would lead to trouble
In relationship and muddle.

Jill Ives

A DONCASTER ADOPTEE

I've got a Yorkshire accent
Doncaster is my *home town*
I'm always glad to get back there
When I've travelled miles around
I go to visit relatives, in far off lands,
And start to get homesick before the holiday ends.

It has an appeal all of its own
Doncaster our famous town
And its butterscotch you should try some
It's so addictive yum, yum, yum
I've travelled the world far and wide
Also England many places I've tried
People say once they hear my *twang*
You're a Yorkshire lass one of the gang
'Where ya from?' Doncaster ay!
We went to their market the other day
I've also lived in Lancashire
Lytham, a smashing place
But to me, Doncaster will always be ace
Many a year I've lived in this town
But, my roots are not home grown
Pembroke is the place I was born
No not Wales, a little further on
But Pembroke Ontario Canada, yes!
But my heart belongs to Doncaster, I guess.

Sandra Witt

MOSQUITO

Look, I'm a generous host but
You've been helping yourself to Bloody Maries
All night long without my permission.
I know, because when I woke up this morning
I was itching without intermission.

What kind of a house guest are you?
You're rude and impolite.
You take without giving anything in return
And then take flight.

I'm growing tired of your softly, softly approach
And the sycophantic way you whine in my ear.
Frankly, your stiletto caresses are bloody painful
And my initial indulgence
Has given way to fear.

From now on there's going to be a different regime.
You'll have to sign the visitor's book in red ink.
And unless I'm feeling unusually hospitable,
You'll pay with your life for the next furtive drink.

Simon Gladdish

A POEM FOR HUMANS

Surely ne'er in human history has there been such ghastly scenes,
Being sent for anyone to see: on all our TV screens,
As the loads of naked bodies being swung or dragged about,
Cadavers of men and women that made me want to shout.

Look! Look! ye milling billions of people on our globe!
See! See! What now awaits us when we are xenophobe!
How long! How long! My people have scenes like these been hid?
Have we been kept in *ignorance* of the *foul things* humans did?'

'Inspired by 'Part world loyalty' instead of teaching all,
To live as *human beings* and be *caring* for us *all*.
See! See! See! ye milling billions, the *ghastly* things which can,
Occur when *we* are brain washed on a *world of peoples* plan.'

Let us *not* blame *one dictator*, alone, for murders made,
It was not *he alone* who planned this holocaust parade.'
It was *error* in the *holy books* which taught us all to be,
The pawns of kings and emperors instead of *one democracy*.

It was preachings from the *God folk*, that we must *kill or die*'
To serve the Ceasars of this world and as *Good Christians* try,
To emulate the *Editor*s who teach us all to say,
My country - oh my country - I will serve *thee* today,

Shun the *popes* and *ayatollahs*, and the fascist war lords crew,
Who *delude themselves* and *all of us* to be war makers too.
We *humans* are the only source of war or peace I know,
There is no *theocratic* source of action here below,

It really is *false teaching* to talk of God at all,
All Gods are myths, so let us say, *'Human Union is our call!'*
Let us build *one global federation* to set all persons free,
To serve *universal unity* and *global democracy*.

Edward Graham Macfarlane

MY SAY

You lift me up so high, so high
I'm as free as a bird I can fly
I'm in a world, a little world of my own
But still within the safety of home
I've travelled the world twice over
Yet never moved from under cover
The blanket under which I hide
Blissfully ignorant to all outside
Sweet mother nature got the upper hand
So follow suit bury your head in the sand
I feel the need to stand and shout
Tell everyone, let my feelings out
But who would listen who would care
You would all look up and stare
And go back from wherever you came
To carry on with this sick, sick game
We all play each and every day
Yes we all know the rules and how to play
But when the time comes who'll say 'I told you so'
For somebody surely must be in the know
The day will almost certainly come
When all the damage is undone
When this world is put to rights
The game is over we've won the fight
But will we ever really be free
When we don't know who holds the key
For when we've all served our sentence
We must try not to hold any vengeance
Just accept what the captor, life hands out
For life is the key there is no doubt.

S Forrester

EASTER

Easter is a time to reflect and to remember
not just an ordinary man, but our God, our
Saviour, Jesus the King.

He was alone on the road carrying a load
a cross twice His size covered him from
His head to His toes. his disciples were
scared and fled as he walked and bled
only His mother stood there with a
disciple named John who thought it
was all through, finished nothing to do.
Nowhere to go.

Hanging there on the cross
He took our sins with His blood.
Then darkness covered the earth
He died to give us new birth.

The next day
Angels appeared
the stone was rolled away.
Nobody was there where Jesus lay
He is risen, He is gone, He is alive.

So as we get ready to celebrate
let's take time out to remember
it is our saviour who gave us
meaning and joy so let's live
life knowing Jesus is in us and
with us, both now and
forevermore.

Nicola Glover-Wright

VOICES

Is there anybody there, listening to me?
Of course there is, them, thee and me!
Insatiable appetites cannot be bought,
They do not behave as they should or ought.

Voices flow from that part of the brain,
Intruding and goading one insane,
Halt! I cry, where's my Jehovah?
Please help me Lord to win them over.

Placate their devious, malicious behaviour,
Help me control them oh! My saviour.
Where art thou God, you have disappeared?
Their ugly heads have again upreared!

V Marsden

THE PYLONS

Pylons march across the hills
supporting high voltage cables,
bringing power to the mills
and hot meals to our tables.

On those slim steel towers
hangs modern civilisation,
they up-hold this culture of ours
and are the life - blood of the nation.

So march on National Power,
over hill and dale you're strung,
on these lattice towers
our consumer cultures hung.

Fred Scott

FISTRAL BAY - EVENING

Jade walls of foam crowned water, unevenly
Parallel surge lemming like
To where sharp sand chews and
Devours them. Yet
As one dies, further out another forms. Like
An inverted "T' a late lone surfer glides
Sideways yet ever shoreward. Far to the
West the last sunbeams dance on embryo
Breakers, the gulls
Wail.

A year ago we two blithely planned to come
Here, but then like an uncaring
Mugger, a merciless God heedless of my pleading tore
Your life from mine, yet still I had to
Come - like the ourfer - alone: A pilgrimage to
Grief, standing among these black crystal
Veined headland rocks the restless green
Deeps below are so
Inviting.

Allen Williams

DENTAL DEPRESSION

I brush my teeth twice, every day but still I suffer tooth decay,
Right now I'm in the waiting room, all deathly hush, all doom and gloom.
The receptionist is full of chat, to *cheer me up*, some hope of that!
But worse, she gives a hearty grin displaying perfect teeth within.
See how they gleam, see how they shine, I wish those pearly whites
were mine.
Then suddenly a thought occurs, I wonder, are they really hers?
Could she be breaking in those teeth for Esther Rantzen or Edward Heath?

But now the time for humour's past, they're calling out my name at last.
I'm through the door, I'm in the chair, oh no, this really isn't fair.
With probe in hand he pokes about until at last I give a shout,
His evil glance confirms the fear, *'One little filling needed there.'*
I stammer back, 'It can't be so. You filled them all six months ago.'
'But just in case it's really true, please, could I beg one thing of you?'
'So I don't suffer undue pain, use lots and lots of lignocaine.'

My mouth grows numb, my knees grow weak, the drill gives out its
ghastly shriek,
With muscles tense and knuckles white I feel the drill bit start to bite.
It grinds, it grates, I curl my toes, that burning smell wafts up my nose,
Then just as I begin to wince he stops and says 'Now have a rinse.'
I sip the mouthwash, swirl it around, spit at the sink and hit the ground,
I lean back in the chair once more and watch the assistant mop the floor.

At last, relief, the deed is done, the filling's in they've had their fun,
I give a big, lopsided smile, convince myself it's all worthwhile.
Yet, as I leave that place behind one thought keeps running through
my mind,
In six months time I'll once again be suffering probing, drilling, pain!

Paul Turner

RATS

Black and brown lumps of fur,
Old stinking rags,
A disease which you cannot escape,
With teeth like razors,
And eyes like pins,
Which stare out from a spiky nose,
Searching for food,
Stealing and destroying,
Whatever they see,
And this terrible thing,
The devils servant,
But we too like them are mammals,
Destroying things around us,
Like rats we scavenge and steal from the earth,
And like rats we don't understand what damage we cause.

Oliver Corder

MY DREAM

I had a dream,
I was in a football team,
We had never lost,
2 million pounds I cost.

Our pitch is great,
People sit on crates,
And when we score,
There's a giant roar.

From what I remember,
I scored in September,
For the greatest team,
But that's only my dream.

Matthew Proud

HEAVEN OR HELL

What do you do
When you come to the end?
Do you pray?
Head down
And try to pretend
Have you thought of the past life
That has been just passed by?

Or do you look at the horror
And stare eye to eye?
Have you thought
Of what might be about?
Have you got frightened
And need someone to give you a shout?

Or have you said your prayers
Morning, noon and night?
And felt confident
To put old nick to flight?
Or have you been
Good, kind, naughty or nice
Or have you been unable
To take good and sound advice?

Or has he tried to tempt you
When you were weak?
Did he fail to get through
As you reached your peak?
These are ordeals that we all go through
But you need to pass them
If you want to be true.

Brian Hale

DO I BELIEVE

For whatever it is worth
we spend our lives upon this earth
all though we suffer pain and grief
some people have a strong belief
and though life's difficult for some
they think there's better things to come.
I know we're only passing through
but just where are we going to?
though I'm only on a visit here
of what's to come I have no fear.
When in the end this life has gone
is there something else to follow on?
There might be a better place to go
but till that time comes I just won't know.

David Howard

TELEVISION

Rejects of soap fame tarnish the music scene
Imports such dismal viewing, it seems
Morning talk shows fraternise
Over sheltered issues then patronise.

Commercials penetrate all
Household products unfold
Catering for material gain
Never ending goods shelved or framed.

Child presenters control studio space
Noticeable hair styles take first place
Without image they hold no face
TV land is where nonsense safe.

Alan Jones

ON MISSING THE LAST BUS

It serves you right, you've missed the bus
You let too many go by
Not quite what you want, you'll wait for the next
Now you're high and dry.

You feel as though you're all alone
The world is passing you by
Not even a ring on the telephone
It makes you want to cry.

Disconsolately gaze through the window
And moodily stare at the rain
Inspiration suddenly strikes you
A way to try again.

On a romantic sea I went sailing
One last fling to try
Weary of all this trailing
A time to do or die.

It was me bomb what done it
The liner sank like a stone
We made it to this island
Me and the Captain alone.

I'm sorry to say, Sue Lawley
It ain't as nice as you think
Stuck with him on this island
With only fresh water to drink.

The moral is, content with yourself
And don't waste time on a dream
It ain't so bad being on the shelf
They're never as good as they seem.

John Potter

LIFE AFTER DEATH

I sleep all day, I sleep all night
I'm dead you see, I got this fright.
I saw the torso of my friend,
Which finally sent me to my end.
My soul in heaven my spirit in hell,
An alarm goes off yet I hear no bell,
Satan whispering in my ears,
About what I've done throughout the years.
The good, the bad, it all comes out,
Now Satan's angry he starts to shout,
You might think you are here to rest,
But you will suffer little pest,
A million years or even more,
Will be terror for you, you little bore,
My God! My God I've lost my cool
Shut up you stupid little fool,
God doesn't want you can't you see,
That's why you were sent here to me,
So I'll keep your spirit alive and well.
Down here in my place known as hell.

William McKechnie

94

EASTER EGGS

The start of the year, our figures look grim
We say to ourselves, 'I really must slim'
So we try very hard to stick to a diet
On times we'll find it's rather a riot
It really needs effort to try not to eat
An occasional cake, biscuit, or sweet.
You start to lose weight, you're happy and glad
And think to yourself, 'Well, it isn't so bad'
Lent comes along. It's much easier then.
Easter is coming, look out ladies and men!
We're given nice eggs, made of nice things
To receive one and eat, oh! what pleasure it brings.
So you're tempted to try and begin to eat
You sit back in sadness, despair and defeat
You think to yourself was my diet in vain?
You joke and you laugh - and begin all again.

Merril Morgan

WHERE WE USED TO DANCE

The full moon's glowing bright white in the sky,
As I sit by the lake where we used to dance.
The question mark sticks close to my mind,
As I wonder . . . Will she show?
Finally the suspense leaves my mind,
As she arrives at the lake where we used to dance.
We sit and talk as the world passes by.

Now hours have passed,
There's just one question that burdens my mind,
Will she stay,
Or will she leave the moonlit lake where we used to dance.

Paul Gildea

AND A LITTLE CHILD SHALL LEAD

From countless light years came the ship, a wingless bird in space,
The remnants of a super world, survivors of a race.
With nothing left, with fuel all spent, with hope and spirits gone,
They cruised through nature's wildness, their prayers were heard as one,
A speck of light, lit by a star, lay on their hapless course,
A risky chance - the great ship turned - a leader's last resource.
With earth in view, a still lush globe, its peoples watched in awe
As silver disc, from painted sky, skimmed high along a shore.
A sun soaked clearing loomed ahead, its white sands filled with grace,
A brilliant flash, a cloud of dust, a final resting place.
The crowds flocked round, the forces came, the quiet was split by thunder,
A buckled hatch, a power inside, the metal ripped asunder.
With bated breath, with weapons raised, with tension near to cracking,
A band of men crouched round the craft, of fear there was no lacking.
Then slowly came the leader out, close followed by his nation,
They did not speak, they stood alone, they faced annihilation.
From countless light years came the ship, through terrors and
                                        through dangers,
To wait their end, a home in sight, and death at the hands of strangers.
The crowd was quiet, the air was still, the men stood face to face,
A nervous man, a frightened man, a helpless alien race.
As seconds passed and no-one spoke and nerves were near to fraying,
A gun was cocked, a clear sharp sound, to mingle with the praying.
Another her sound, much closer now, strained faces looked about,
Then from the crowd, a little girl, a joyous childish shout,
With arms outstretched, with face aglow, she held her latest toy,
A friendly gift, a loss to her, but life for an alien boy.
For as she handed him this gift, a barrier had been broken,
His smile said all there was to say, not a single word was spoken.
A friendship aura, bright and clear, spread rapidly around,
A welcomed noise, relief indeed, as weapons hit the ground.
No longer fear, no longer hate, of this there was no need,
For even the Holy Bible says, 'And a little child shall lead.'

J Crompton

THE JACK FROST BITE

He creeps up so slyly and makes not a sound
Dodging the wet paving stones on the cold ground
With a flick of his fingers and a click of his heels
He covers the whole street with iced diamond weal's
Beware the Jack Frost bite and the sting in his tail
For many have laughed lightly at this fairy tale

But others have known better and lived to regret
The demon from Iceland who shows no respect
That he kisses the trees with his icicle breath
And covers their leaves in a snow white death
He leaves no mercy and only evokes fear
We pray to the almighty that he will disappear

As the months go by heat saps his strength
His knobbly iced fingers shrink in great length
The long white body is now no more than a big ball
How much do we fear this pathetic like lump and give
It a swift kick in its hefty white rump.

Amber Nair

BLACK AND WHITE

Dark were the hands that lay
Begrimed and grey
In the sweat of the day.

Ebony embers burn,
In ire's urn,
Tireless toil,
African soil.

Caught in the net
Prejudice yet
Heaven or hate?
Ironic embrace.

Separateness
To bless
You and I
Neath the same sky.

'Give me your hand?'
Black is banned
Silent they stand.

Different yet akin
Simply the colour of the skin
One, yet not the same
Apartheid's pain.

Do not despair
Deeply hidden there
Spiritual light,
Ignite
The Brotherhood of Black and White.

Rita Brisk

FOR THE LOVE OF THE LIFE GIVER

Teachers teach teachers - from the learners -
Who are teachers,
The stripping of the Masters to the bone.
For the answers as to who were the very first creatures
Or who was the first - alone!
Pupils borne pupils, in the hope they are chosen
As the sacrifice to represent good,
But might not the answer be below the ice frozen
Or deeper still, betwixt once blooming wood?

The labyrinth of nature is for both pupils and teachers -
But to go nowhere, except where, they are told.
Likewise applies to both the preached and the preachers
By the greatest life story ever sold!
Both teachers and preachers, ' yes men', such lowly creatures -
They see a sacrifice before the scarified.
For the man who goes nowhere with such ghostlike features
Ends up like always, by being crucified!

Robert Kilpatrick

A CHRISTMAS CARROT

Dinner round at my Bleak House Mother's
Great Expectations of Hard Times for the meal
Telling her Tale of Two Turkeys
Like a Christmas Carrot I'll feel

Christmas Blight
Scrooge was right
Bah Humbug

It's the first year I've missed Midnight Mass
Missed Lewis's Santa as well
Still, I've not had to fix the tree fairy lights
But it's the first year Christmas is Hell!

Christmas Blight
Scrooge was right
Bah Humbug

Christmas morning here in my bedsit
Thoughts of kids opening presents with glee
Laughing round at their Mother's
Still warm in the envelope - my decree

Christmas Blight
Scrooge was right
Bah Humbug.

Dennis Conlon

THE MOTORWAY

The large machines that scrape the earth,
The bulldozers so strong.
Changing the face of the countryside,
Building a roadway so long.

Lorries all full to the brim with earth,
Scraped from a long wide line.
A wood that fell to a woodman's axe,
Gone with never a sign.

Concrete and stone, gravel and tar,
A roller to roll smooth and hard.
The big signs erected now and again,
Keeping you all on your guard.

And so as the days and the months slip by,
This scar looking almost snow white.
Is a motorway bright in the morning sun,
A road way that runs out of sight.

A B Hughes

ADORATION

He lay in his hammock, under the trees,
enjoying the beautiful day,
When she tentatively moved over to him,
in her slinky seductive way.

What a beautiful creature you are, he said,
you move with such ease and grace,
So she nestled her head on his shoulder,
And gazed lovingly into his face.

But I'm neglecting my duties,
You're bound to be hungry by now,
Then she gently placed her cheek against his,
As she uttered a soft meow.

Florence M Vass

LOVE IS LIKE A SUNNY DAY

Hello love,
Hello sunshine,
As sweet as a dove,
Flying over in springtime.
A beautiful day,
With clouds a blue,
The air is sweet,
Because I love you,
As I love you more and more each day,
And I'll never let your love slip away,
Because your love is like a sunny day,
And I hope it will be here to stay,
As happiness can be,
Now that you are here with me.

Emma Kemm

MEMORIES

Close one's mind, shut one's eyes,
See fluffy clouds a floating by,
Smell the scent of new mown grass,
Please let this moment last.

The warm summer sun, a gentle breeze,
These things I remember with ease,
A stroll on the beach, I remember too,
Arms entwined, just me and you.

Watching the sun set in the sky,
The seagulls flying upon high,
The sky like velvet, black and dark,
The same as I feel now, in my heart.

What happened to the love we had?
Was it destroyed by circumstance?
Or did it take its course and die?
No, it died because of mistakes we made.

Time will erase the hurt, the pain,
Like dirt washed by the rain,
But the memories, they will stay,
Within my heart, for many a day.

V Woodhouse

THE COUNTRY

As you walk down a country lane
Have you ever stopped to look
At all the wonderful things around you
Such as the trees
And the babbling brook

On either side there may be fields of grass
Where the cows are put to graze
Oh there may even be a wood
With its paths winding like a maze

Further along the country lane
You might see a farmhouse
With its whitewashed walls
And a faithful sheepdog at the gate
Ready to get the sheep in before night falls

Next time you're in the country
Just think about these things
And take notice of the things around you
And you will realise how wonderful it is.

Betty Glave

THINGS ARE A-CHANGING

When I look around my home town things they are a-changing.
Town Hall, brewery all knocked down things they are a-changing.
No more ship yard, no more pit,
Lo-Cost opens, Co-operative split.
Things they are a-changing.
No more cinema, just a club,
Precinct's open, shop's boarded up.
Things they are a-changing.
No more pool in the park, no more monkey run in the dark,
No more swing bridge fly over lark.
Things they are a-changing.
Market day four times a week, where the shoppers like to meet,
You can see the stalls from my old street.
Things they are a-changing.
The school I attended privately owned,
The vicarage, a residential home.
Things they are a-changing.
Doctor's surgery all in one, no Sally Army singing their songs,
Most of the people have long gone.
Things they are a-changing.
No more cottage where I was born just an empty space,
The old folks' centre over the road and then a parking place.
Things they are a-changing.
But when I look back up our street where things have been a-changing,
I see the church just the same and I think it's quite amazing.

Shirley Ann Quinn

NOSTALGIC MOMENTS

Land of hope and glory, they robustly sang
And waving banners at the Proms until the rafters rang,
How nostalgic and loyal we all feel,
If only those times would come back to heal,
Our hearts cry out and long for the day
When there was law and order and crime didn't pay,
And the old were safe, not robbed and battered,
Being healthy and happy was all that mattered.
When we look back to that peaceful time,
All the intervening years of drugs and crime,
What went wrong? To find ourselves in today's position?
Something must have been very lax in transition,
The punishment used to fit the crime?
Now they are sent abroad to have a good time.
The judicial system has all gone to pot,
The sentences and excuses; a lot of utter rot.
Must we bring back hanging, hard labour, and the birch?
Severely punish the offenders, before others are besmirched.

B Pim

I LIKE A REAL GOOD BOOK

I'm very fond of reading, I like a real good book,
And if I only had my way, I'd sooner read than cook,
Those long romantic novels, with the hero in full cry,
The villain in the boudoir, who snarls 'Submit or die!'
Those westerns in the desert, the Indians on the trail,
The sheriff who keeps getting shot, but you know he cannot fall.

Those convoys in the forties, when we won world war two,
The handsome captain on the bridge, who always saw them through.
The jewel thief *par excellence*, of course his name is Raffles;
The inspector, down from Scotland Yard, who he always baffles,
That drama in the hospital, when the surgeon wields that knife,
The charming sister on the ward, who makes a lovely wife.

The RAF in wartime, soaring with the *few*,
The bombings and the blackouts and a *wizard prang* or two.
Adventures in the prison camps - Colditz and *Wooden Horse;*
Tunnelling out to freedom, with the stars to set their course.
The spies who drop by parachute and contact the resistance,
The battles with the Gestapo, as they radio for assistance.

The *private eye* who steps right in, where angels fear to tread,
He's searching for that missing girl, who ends up in his bed!
Those squeamish *meaty* dramas about the kitchen sink,
They're hardly entertainment, but they sure do make you think.

Now I come to think of it, my life's been like a book,
That tells the old, old story, with a faintly tattered look.
If I could just go back again and start afresh, my friend,
The story might be different, but I wonder how it would end?

Robert Arthur Markland

WINTER TRAINING

It's that time of season again when training's in full flow,
When you'd rather stay in bed, than go out in rain or snow.
The bike's been sitting there, while you've enjoyed your fun,
Now's the time for wind and rain, forget about the sun!
Out comes the jacket, thermal leggings, hat and mitts,
And then there's the waterproof and overboots to cover the other
Bits.
The face is either blank or grimacing as down the road you go
The legs - I think - are going round, but the pedalling's very slow
I'm sick of getting half way there, and suddenly getting wet
As the rain falls down real steady, and the mud begins to set.
Not only on your hat and face but always up your back
My bike it is a beacon - for finding water, it's got the knack.
Why do I get mud splattered leggings that go right up to my seat?
While the puddles run like rivers as they squelch out from my feet.
But still *we* sit here peddling, rain running off our chin
Suffering all the elements, to get some training in.
Sometimes we have some company, to lighten up the pace -
But all that brings is another wheel to splash muck up in your face.
The wind it bites your ears and blows you almost flat
Wrestling and struggling with the bike, when oh! So precariously sat.
Every push on the crank is an effort when crabbing side to side,
Who else would be out in this! As round the bends you slide.
But you'd be surprised how many idiots like me out there you'd get
Doing the trials and tribulations of training in the wet.
Us cyclists are real crazy, to get like this we're shattered,
But what I'm really trying to say is - in fact - we're really knackered.
And if the rain doesn't get you, on this you can depend -
Is a great big whacking juggernaut storming round the bend
Who gives you plenty of room - then cuts you up instead,
And sends a tidal wave crashing over your head!
Which slowly filters down your back and spreads across your
Shoulder
And what with the soggy bum as well, even makes you feel much
Colder.

As my reddened face gets beaten, by the ever bouncing hail
I've got weary bone syndrome, as I'm hitting the homeward trail.
And as I'm getting nearer I at last can force a laugh
'Coz you're still out there, and I'm inside - in a well earned Radox
Bath.

Sue Bonning

ALE OF A TALE

Stone faced stands the Griffin
Comfy chairs thou to sit in
Over the road the Sow and Pig's
To Recontrer for cigs and swigs

Sign of the Crown selling cheap grog
A ratcatcher sits sipping cider with his dog
Singing choirboys at the Angel Inn
The vicar don't mind it isn't a sin

They say at Christmas it's jolly good fun
Heads are sozzled at the Old Sun
Across the green to the Old Red Lion
Morris men dance to an accordion

Bells from the church greet the Oddfellow's Arms
Masonic meetings drowned by the psalms.
Along the street the Nag's Head beckons
A bloody good pint the roadsweeper reckons.

Red coated huntsmen spinning some good yarns
Waited on by busty maidens the meet at Bedford Arms.
Beer and wine whisky and gin
Devil's Disciples hold court at Bell Inn

Dennis Cox

ANOTHER NOTION - ANOTHER WHIM

I like to make things out of wood,
To keep at it daily, I really should,
It starts with great gusto and with great vigour.
My expectations get bigger and bigger,
It went from wood, to painting china,
There really can't be anything finer,
But that was also put aside,
When it should have been finished, and displayed with pride,
Wielding the knife - the paintbrush - the thread,
I think I'll bake a cake instead,

They are all in cardboard boxes, and carrier bags
There's even a half finished rug made from rags,
Another notion, another whim
They'll probably end up in the bin,
But one day I'll bring them down from the attic,
And persevere and try to attack it.

Anne McWilliams

LADY CLOG DANCER'S LAMENT

Oh dear! My poor aching feet.
I've got to keep up with the beat.
On my face there's a smile
But in spite of that I'll
Be dead if I don't find a seat.

Oh dear! My poor aching wrists.
They can't cope with the swivels and the twists
Of the garland, or flicks
Of the bell-laden sticks.
I would hide but I'm bound to be missed.

Oh dear! My poor aching toes.
On and on the accordion goes.
Spare time's catered for
By hobbies galore.
Why's clog dancing the one that I chose?

Muriel Noton

MY PERFECT DAY

Breakfast in bed would start the day
My eggs cooked in a certain way.
Then, I'd lie in a perfumed bath
With no-one to hear me sing or laugh.
Plenty of time to open the post
Letters and parcels - things I like most.
A day at the *sales* would be a great treat,
Stopping only for lunch and to rest my feet.
A large plate from the salad bar, gammon ham, thick and lean,
Almond cake, cappuccino - a meal for a Queen!
Until the last boutique closed more bargains I'd find
Leaving the evening for a chance to unwind.
Dainty tea by the fireside, just enough time to read
My favourite woman's journal - then a warm bed I'd need !!!

Diana Cole

ODE TO A POET

I'm a poet
And don't I
Know it!
I simply
Can't wait
To show it!
Needing
Neither reason
Or a rhyme!
I just cannot
Wait to shine!
People yawn
From time to time!
But I know that
I'm doing
Just fine!

Catherine B Parness

STARDREAMING

How I love to see the sky at night
And wonder at the stars so bright
To see the moon so far away
And let my imagination run astray
How I wish to be an astronaut
But being only eight I'm too short
How I'd love to fly among the stars
To be the first boy to set foot on Mars
The stars shine and sparkle
Even the midnight fox stops to marvel
My spaceship would swoop and dive
From adventure I would never hide
I'd discover planets in the milky way
And have adventures every day
I hope this day comes very soon
To be the first boy on the moon.

Antony Clarke

MY HOBBY

Wee Willie Winkie lives with me,
So does *Red Riding Hood* too.
Little Miss Muffet sits on her tuffet,
Smiling at *Little Boy Blue*
.
Mary Mary quite contrary,
Carries her watering can.
Jack and Jill sit quite still,
As do *Alice* and *Peter Pan.*

Little Jack Horner sits in the corner,
Wondering what he can do.
Lucy Locket looks in her pocket,
To search for a sweet or two.

Next to them sit lovely ladies,
Dressed in elegant gowns.
And some kings and queens,
Dancers and circus clowns.

Then come soldiers and sailors,
With a bevy of pretty girls.
Bonnie babies, with finest faces,
And hair in cutest curls.

Some can walk, some can talk,
Others just sit all day,
One or two say 'Mama',
Some would like to play.
A few of them are musical,
One or two are trolls.
The mystery has now been solved,
For all of them are *dolls!*

Eugenie Barker

FUN AND GAMES

Pastimes and hobbies, there is many a choice,
Whatever your leaning, its a time to rejoice,
Perhaps when you stand on the oche, with one last dart,
Could it be its a double top finish, that's nearest your heart.

Perhaps you prefer billiards, or is snooker your call,
The audience wait with baited breath, on the table the last ball,
Your cue is ready poised, an eagle eye and steady aim,
While all are nervous around you, one more winning game.

Table tennis may be your choice, with a spin on your serve,
As you keep returning service, with concentration and nerve,
One final swing of the arm, a smash of that elusive white ball,
You now have advantage point, instead of twenty all.

Maybe you are a painter, of water colours or oils,
Creating greens, blues and reds, or browns of the soil,
Bring scenes of life to your canvass, an artistic keen gift,
While others admire your artistry, it can give them a lift.

Those days in your garden, planting seeds in the soil,
Summer follows springtime, plants and flowers grow so tall,
Birds and animals visit, and partake in this charm,
You create a beautiful natural order, away from life's harm.

Strolling and walking in the countryside, or along the seashore,
Rambling happily with your loved ones, who could ask for more,
Green trees, fields and hedgerows, alive with birds and working bee,
Or seaweed mingling with jellyfish, and calming sounds of the sea.

Whatever your callings, be they activities indoors or out,
Partaking in and enjoying them, is what it is really about,
May you continue to find new interest, of laughter in the sun,
And if you've a notion, let others join in and have fun.

Jim Wilson

NOTHING GREAT

I've flown many a kite by day and at night
And I've had many pleasures at an airshow sight.

I used to fish and many happy hours have had
And played hop-scotch and conkers as a lad.

I can't boast of anything great
Yet I've known happiness and a mate.

Other sports I have played in my mind
But only so because the money I could not find.

I've even felt the air rush past me in the sky
But there are some pastimes and hobbies that I wouldn't even try.

Why should this ever be so?
Could it be no money no nerve no guts to have a go?

But don't rush to place your bet
The old boy might have a go yet!

Clive Cornwall

SPRING

Spring is the time I love!
Blue skies hovering above
The birds singing their song
Dark nights not so long -
New leaves on the trees
Buds starting to open
Getting ready for the bees
The sun starting to shine
Makes you feel fine!
Hanging baskets must be filled
To make a lovely show
And off to Chelsea to have a go
Spring is in the air!
I'll show my basket if I dare
Win the gold or just a share
I can but dream
They are so rare -
It is only spring in the air!

Kathleen Peebles

A FOOTBALL GAME

Every once in a while, with my husband, to the football ground we go.
Myself, to eye up the players, himself, to get involved with the show.

Each integral move is noted as my husband studies the game.
Watching with keen devotion, as with the players I do the same.

Now the goal-keeper's rather dishy in his multi-coloured top and black cap.
The crowd seem to think he's no good. Who cares? With looks like that!

The home team is attacking, with ball passing so accurate and slick.
The cross comes in, the crowd rise to their feet, and the striker is poised
Ready to kick.

But defender is there with a tackle, and he and the striker collide.
The striker goes down, in his once clean kit which now has mud all down
One side.

The referee looks to his linesman who waves his flag around his ears.
Which apparently means it's a goal kick, but the crowd has other ideas.

'Borrow my glasses' they shout at the linesman, as gradually they start to
Sit down.
And 'The referee's a w*****!' rings out all over the ground.

Meanwhile, the away side is attacking, they've run forward on the break.
Next thing I know, a goal has been scored, and I missed it by mistake.

I'm too busy watching the crowd and the substitutes warming up.
But to miss a goal, even by the opposition, well, that's just my luck!

Just one minute of time is remaining. Now the final whistle blows.
The away side are the victors. Sometimes that's just the way it goes!

But I am unable to console my husband. He feels his side deserved to win.
They did have the best looking players. 'But it's only a game,' I remind
him!

Peta C C Vale

FORTUNES

I have many hobbies -
One thing I'll gladly do,
If you cross my hand with silver
I'll *tell the cards* for you.

First, just sit in comfort,
Relax and clear your mind
While I consult the Tarot
And see what I can find.

The pack I cut precisely
In piles one to three
And each pile contains your secrets
All laid out there for me.

Is it love or money
Which is your heart's desire?
I can promise you a fortune
If that's what you require.

Then there are the tea leaves
This can be very nice
I can see a handsome stranger
In tea bags - at a price!

Or if you prefer it
There is another way
Any article if handled
Your future can relay.

I will bring you romance
And happiness and wealth
Or if you're *really* lucky
I'll promise you good health!

Molly Stone

SMALL IS BEAUTIFUL

A pastime? A hobby? It's neither of those!
It's a lifetime's obsession as I will disclose.
A wondrous obsession! A fantasy and . . .
But come, share it with me! Take hold of my hand.

Imagine you're shrinking. It's not hard, so try
To pretend you are no more than six inches high.
That done, off we go! I'll show you the way
Round my diminutive world where all work is play.

Shall we visit the butcher, greengrocer and baker?
Pop into the pub for a lager and lime?
There's a darts game in progress in one of the bar-rooms
And here, at *The Cock*, the landlord never calls *time*.

Should you need a new frock for that special occasion
Call at *Just Looking,* the ladies' boutique.
But if it's golfclubs you're after; a football or ice-skates,
Smallsports is open seven days of the week.

Mr Brown at the pet shop, is busy as ever
Weighing out Spillers' Shapes from an over-full sack.
See the hamsters and mice in the window display
And the birds in the aviary down at the back?

Meantime down at the market stallholders are calling,
Encouraging folk to sample their wares
Cheeses, wood-turnings, bunches of flowers -
Just look at the shine on those apples and pears!

Do you enjoy lobster, winkles or crab?
The shellfish are fresh - and ever will be -
But if such produce is not to your liking
Let's buy fish 'n' chips to take home for our tea!

Your short visit's over. Permission to grow!
I'll stay small a while longer - I love it here so!

Judith Eleanor Landry

AUTUMN WOODS

Bracken now begins to dim
And turns from green to foxy brown
While rushy grass and dying bramble
Touches dock and thistledown.
Butterflies will play no longer
Nature sends them all away,
Baby fledglings learnt to fly,
Though I see none of these today,.
I walk alone or run beside
Wild hops and coloured leaves that hide
Between thin stems of pale fireweed
That sports a fluffy head of seed.
I see blackberries, elder fruits,
Fungus grow from crooked roots,
Reddish toadstools stand besidde
Russet leaves and flowers that died.
A yellow hammer, happy, sings,
A pigeon flusters flaps his wings,
The yew boughs spread, the chestnut bends
Above the brown leaf path that wends,
I stand beneath and stretch to reach
The roughened mast on bough of beech,
I gather cones, rose hips and haws,
Or spindle with pink orange claws,
And though it saddens me when precious
Autumn sunlight dims,
I smile again for spring awaits
As winter time begins.

Audrey Keen

MY GARDEN AND I

My garden is my forte
It takes most of my spare time
I'll disappear for hours
In this magical world of mine.
It's where I sit and philosophy
Over worries care and strife
Analyse each and every problem
And take on a different view of live.

I am a lover of beauty and nature
So my garden is special to me
It's the only place on earth
I can feel entirely free.
Each little task that I perform
Is never a waste of time
It's a rung on the ladder of life
In this magical world of mine.

When cutting the lawn or pruning a tree
I'm cutting the pain from my heart
When planting bulbs, flowers or seeds
I'm giving life a brand new start.
I trust my garden with my secrets
Contemplate the world at length
It answers me with it's beauty
So I retain an inner strength.

If I spend all my life-time
Every second of my birth
I will never be able to repay
All this beauty here on earth!

June Madeline Archer

FISHING

Sat in scenic splendour
The angler waits stone still;
With statuesque endeavour,
Oblivious to the chill.
In frozen contemplation
Against an unseen prey,
Devoid of perspiration
This is the game to play.
Astride his rodded barrel
Fish sniper sights his float;
But day long not a ripple
From the foe beneath the boat.
Beaten by baneful billows
And not one bloater bitten -
By the celebrating shallows
The failed fisherman is smitten.
Stare dazed, the day now done
And scales of justice empty,
The fish had clearly won
Their anonymity.
In finless agitation -
Free supper now denied -
The foamy fathomer's portion
A fish-bar will provide!

John Mayer

GOLF

Take up golf the doctor said,
You'll get fresh air and clear your head
So off to the course I did haste
Not wanting precious time to waste

I brought the clubs I brought the balls
And rushed to join the other fools
On the first tee I made a hash
Missing the ball with my first slash

On the second I started to hit it clean
It only took fourteen strokes to reach the green
My putting stroke was elementary
I finished the hole on under twenty

At the third I did falter
Putting eighteen balls into the water
But I got across in the end
With the use of a boat and a diver friend

At the fourth I looked quite good
Until I topped my ball into the wood
Getting it out I'll leave unspoken
Enough to say several clubs were broken

I dashed back to the nineteenth hole
My nerves in shreds out of control
I saw my doctor at the bar
And set about making him under par.

John Ainger

MEMORIES

Thank you for the kind words that
once made my day,
Thank you for keeping in touch in
your own special way.
I wish we could turn the
clock back,
and remember when we first met.
Especially the happy moments
I shall never forget.
Maybe one day we will find the
time to truly make amends
and all them unsaid words of
love will come out in the end.
But if we never manage
that,
There's one thing I must say,
the love that blossomed
months ago
is glowing still today.

Roseanne Dunn

THE DENTIST

Lie back, relax, the spotlight bright
Burns deep into my eyes
While figure in white and mask above
Responsive to my cries
Open wide, the probing starts
The problem's just in here
Won't hurt a bit the muffled voice
Just deepens hidden fear
Cutters, needles, pointed tools
Clamps and things in steel
The torture chamber's instruments
To hand, this can't be real
I know my jaw's been aching mad
I felt I'd go insane
No sleep, can't eat, the nagging throb
The everlasting pain
Give anything to make it stop
To make it go away
But that was yesterday at home
I'm in the chair today
Compelled I was to climb the stairs
Enter the room of hell
The lesser of two evils calls
Now all will soon be well
Behind the mask the dentist smiles
The numbing drug injected
That paralyses half my face
All tissue is affected
Heaven, relief, the pain has stopped
It's time to have his fun
No time to shout, I've changed my mind
The drilling has begun.

J W Wallace

A GARDEN

A garden that gives us
So much pleasure
Trees and shrubs
And plants that we treasure.

Then comes the spring
Planting seeds,
Raking the soil
Pulling up weeds.

June with her roses
And sweet smelling flowers,
In a garden we spend
Many happy hours.

Birds in the trees
Busy with their nests
Helping to rid us
Of garden pests.

With watering can busy
The sun's long rays
And lots of fresh air
Many halcyon days.

Anne Cadwallender

PEDALLING POWER

Some may swim and some may hike,
But my greatest joy is off on my bike.
Wind a blowing, rain a driving,
Pumping, panting, yet still thriving.

A dear old man rides past each day,
Legs pummel slowly on his way -
Gives a knowing nod and a secret smile
Which says we are able to pedal awhile.

It's a special society, a breed apart,
Pedalling power is good for the heart!

Jeremy on his up hill climbs,
Silver racers with gleaming lines.
Not really sitting on razor saddles,
Waddling up hill in straddles.
Panting, beating, feeling half dead,
Sweating, shaking and legs like lead.
Feel like their guts are bursting with heat,
A mighty effort - yet victory's sweet.

Glory blazing in their eyes,
A breed apart you realise!

D M Cudmore

HOOKED ON BOOKS

Books are my one great passion
I love every one I possess
My shelves are crammed full of all wonderful works
There's no room for much else I confess
I've the poems of Milton and Shelley
Alongside John Masefield and Keats
While Bunyon and Robert L Stevenson
Rub shoulders with tales of great feats
On the top shelf encyclopaedias stand
Majestic they look - full of poise
My study looks more like a library
(So much so - that I won't allow noise)
Shakespeare and Dickens take pride of place
Beside Pepys and George Bernard Shaw
If I acquire many more I shall run out of space
And begin stacking them on the floor
There are stories of exploration
And the heroes of all the great wars
There are books on nature and cookery
And all the old and new laws
My friends all assume I must have a great mind
With all of this knowledge around
To tell you the truth my interest lies
In the way that the books are bound
For all the adventurous tales of great lovers
Not a word have I read -
I simply just love the covers

Joan Brown

CIRCUS

Kids and cats and acrobats.
Sawdust, music and swings.
Painted faces all around.
And trousers tied up with string.

Long legs that pace about.
And fire thrown into the air.
Balls that dance like butterflies.
Then clowns which come in pairs.

Dogs who bark and frolic about.
Popcorn, fizzy drinks and sweets.
Hoops thrown up ever so high.
And tier upon tier of seats.

Clowns who throw water and other things.
The trapeze which soars in the heights.
Ponies prancing and trotting around.
And ladies with feathers and tights.

A huge great tent with stripy walls.
Cheers and laughter from everyone.
Juggling, balancing and plates that spin.
All the children having such fun.

Hats, red noses and coloured hair.
The ring master in his suit.
Tumbling men on trampolines.
And great big shiny boots.

Chattering monkeys dressed up in clothes.
All that can be done is shown.
The finale is the best of it all.
And then it's time to go home.

S L Coutts

DREAM TRIP

I do enjoy travel
Be it train, coach or car
Whether round local towns
Or to cities afar.

I've travelled on ferries
A gondola too
And a helicopter trip
Was a fun thing to do.

I've ridden an elephant
In the far east
Rode a big Harley Davidson
That was a beast!

I've taken a ski lift
To snow capped heights
Coached across deserts
Seen wonderful sights.

I've flown in small airplanes
And huge jumbos too
But before I'm much older
There's a thing I must do.

My ambition is not
To fly to the moon
But to float through the air
In a hot air balloon.

Judy Watson

DREAM OR REALITY - PANTO COMES TO RHYL

4 am already, I could hardly open my eyes,
I was dreaming of a land where gorgeous girls were guys,
Where people wore glass slippers, and old men dressed as young ladies,
And little black rats turned into cute little ponies - it all seemed so crazy!

I left before sunrise, I was still in a daze,
Travelling to the west, where I'm told, dragons still laze,
Darkness had fallen, finally Rhyl was is my sights
My coach driver dumped my bags in a puddle, without even a friendly
'goodnight'.

My hotel, I think, stretched the truth - they printed a lie
The *only 5 minutes walk away* seemed like 20 I cry,
Struggling in the howling wind, my bags had a mind of their own,
The freezing bombardment of rain was trying to stop me from reaching
'home'.

Coffee, showered and changed, I was eager to go,
Determined to fight the elements, I was going to the ball, (I mean show).
I headed for the beacon of light, like a stranded ship heading for safety,
The theatre finally in my grasp, why couldn't life be easy.

I felt a little out of my depth, as I waded through the sea of *dwarfs*
T'was like being a tree in a poppyfield, or that skyscraper in Canary Wharf,
The littleuns, sucking their thumbs in anticipation of what the evening
could bring
Clutching their fairy wands, and photos of the Prince and Dandini (the
ex-Neighbours twins).

Tales of poverty, and wicked sisters too,
Poor old cinders had it hard with so much work to do,
Time to let her hair down was only in her dreams,
But good friend Buttons cheered her up - he had designs on her it seems!

A kaleidoscope of events changed her destiny,
Bumping into Prince Charming - whose voice denied his masculinity!
Cupid's arrow was truly struck, oh how the angels sang,
He lost her, but got Cinders back, just like a boomerang.

Peter Dyer

BOBBY C

Four am alarm bells ring
and out of bed we get
fishing tackle in the car
and don't forget the net.
We travelled miles to reach the pond
the sun now rising high
it's a lovely summer morn
the clouds are drifting by.
Now it's time to settle down
and put the bait on hook
cast it in the water
now we will try our luck.
Float is now a bobbing
adrenaline's at its height
float has gone right under
At last we've got a bite.
We make our strike
the hook is set
we play the fish
into the net
fish now caught
our task is done
it's time to travel back.

Another brilliant day we've had,
Both me and brother Jack.

John Longstaff

THE LP'S LAMENT

Techno advances have come a long way,
Since rock *n* rolls first forty-five,
So here lies my ode to the trusty long play,
In attempt to keep it's memory alive.

I'll miss the crackle as the needle touched down,
Just one order - first song to final,
I'll miss the gatefold sleeve, free posters and dust,
The picture discs and rare yellow vinyl.

The engineer's messages scratched into wax,
And Roger Dean's fantasy lands,
I'll miss inner sleeves, I think, most of all,
With printed lyrics and photos of bands.

Black twelve-inch platters have seen good and bad,
It's a daunting task I must risk,
To my three-hundred albums I must bid farewell,
As I convert them all to compact disc!

Garen Ewing

RAMBLERS

On a Saturday morning the ramblers will go
Out for a walk in the rain or the snow
To learn all about the wild things in life
They go out in groups or as husband and wife
Or with someone else if they so choose
And take along with them an old pair of shoes
To walk through the woods to hear the birds sing
And to study the leaves it's an interesting thing

They will walk by the river and watch the fish swim
And take notes of each outing maybe put it on film
For a hobby that takes you out and about
Meet up with the ramblers and you will find out
More about wildlife than you ever thought
'Cause they know it all with the knowledge they've got
They will pass information to young and to old
And in the evening return to the fold

They'll invite you all back next Saturday morning
And you'll be up with the lark half asleep and still yawning
But once you get out in the fresh open air
You won't be too worried about the state of your hair
It will blow in the wind maybe even get wet
And by evening you'll need a shampoo and a set
So if you are fond of the outdoors just take a gamble
Why not join the club and go for a ramble?

Jessie Chestnutt

TEA

When I wake up in the morning
There's only one thing I want you see
It's always very simple
And it means so much to me.

Nothing else will ever do
It's all I ever need
And really, until I've had it
I won't wake up. That's me!

As soon as I open my eyes
I think of nothing more
It's all that I want and need
And I tell you that for sure.

The very thought of it
Makes me smile and grin
Well, it really turns me on
Is that okay, It's not a sin.

Doesn't matter who you are
Just do this one thing for me
Go and put the kettle on
And make a cup of tea.

Beverley Rose

SUMMER HOLIDAY

Let's go inside and buy some rock -
This cold east wind is quite a shock.
You can't have a spade and bucket yet
Because the beach is much too wet;
I know you'd get wet in the sea,
But drenched with rain is all I'd be.
No, it's more than just a shower -
I wish this place had Blackpool Tower.
We'll have some fish and chips quite soon -
It may be dry this afternoon.
Let's get the next sight-seeing bus -
Do go inside without a fuss.
I know you're fed up with the shops,
But you've had lots of chocolate drops.
A nice cream tea is what I'd like.
Yes, I wish too, you'd got your bike.
Now, after tea, let's try the pier -
But then, it's much more sheltered here.
Still too wet to do my knitting' -
Wish we had a car to sit in!
Let's have a drink to drown our sorrow;
The weather may be good tomorrow.

Dorothy Roberts

LAST WORDS

What immortal words of mine
Could frame a publishable line?
No digressions from the theme,
Making first a careful scheme.
Cut out all verbosity,
Don't show precocity.
Aim to please the average reader,
Or you'll never write the leader
In the glossies of the day,
For which you then can make them pay.
Can I write a Mills and Boone,
With romance, glamour, moon and June,
For Dollar, Yen and Kruger Rand
And tax exile in Switzerland?
Or should I try a different plane
And write an obscure work, to gain,
In this intellectual guise,
The much disputed Booker Prize?
I fear my skills are suited more
For *Letters to the Editor*.
My master-piece will ne'er be writ,
So let this be my own 'Obit'!

B Gordon

A FISHERMAN'S LIFE

A fisherman's life is a wonderful life
When relaxing by the water,
Doing the things that he likes to do
And not doing the things he ought'a,
Through rain and snow and sunshine
He'll be sitting by the river,
Waiting for the float to sink
And for the rod to start to quiver.

In weeds and reeds and beneath the trees
He will sit and wait,
For that once in a lifetime *big fish*
To come and take his bait,
And when he eventually hooks it
With one almighty yank,
He will be the proudest man
Upon the river bank.

And when the day is over
And all is said and done,
He will tell his family
How he fought the fish and won,
And as the night is closing
He'll lay down his head and dream
Of the excitement and tranquillity
Of the ever peaceful stream.

Alan Pine

THE FISHING TRIP

Off you went, to try to achieve,
Catching a cod, to make me believe,
That you could do it, no problems at all,
Catching a cod, whether big or small,
You were determined to have another go,
To catch that cod, so you could show,
Me that it's possible, to bring one home,
Instead of coming, home alone,
So you arranged, to go out in a boat,
A few miles out, you then went afloat,
Cast the line out, as far as it would go,
Nothing yet happening, the water moved slow,
To your amazement, a tug on the line,
Reeling in, all seemed to be fine,
With your excitement, you pulled out the cod,
Oh! what a beauty, at the end of the rod,
You couldn't lift him, for he was heavy,
Into the boat, you brought him in steady,
He was long and fat, and he should please,
Her indoors, she can no longer tease
Me anymore that, I can't catch a fish,
Here I've got a cod, for a main dish,
Your friends will be envious, over you,
You can go again, if you want to,
But you must bring a cod home everytime,
Make it worth your while, and mine.

Lynn Hallifax

GOLF

When I play golf, it gives me pleasure,
It really is a game of leisure.
I now prepare, to use my *driver*,
'God', I wish the fairways were wider.
Please have some manners, when I tee off,
Whatever you do, please don't cough.
It could put me off, and make me *slice*,
I don't think that, would be very nice.
On the other hand, I might also *hook*,
I read that somewhere, in a book.
And as I play, I shout out 'fore',
There goes another *double boggy* onto my score.
Would you believe it, I'm in the sand,
I really do need, a helping hand.
I take a *sand wedge*, to get me out,
But once again, it's 'fore' I shout.
This really is not a good day,
another *ball* has gone astray.
Would you believe it, I missed the *green*,
There goes another *ball*, never to be seen.
But I hope before my days are done,
That I might *sink*, a *hole in one*.

John Henry Pritchard

CARTOPHILY

Fairest is the flower that shines from thee,
a *Kensitas* silk upon my knee,
What is that? you may ask,
a *Cartophilic* item from the past.

Woven and printed, canvas too,
paper, plastic and card, animals in the zoo.
Miniature rugs from the US of A
metal badges and shaped flags, from first war days.

First aid, air raid, Do-you-know? milkmaid,
card games, famous Dames, poultry, family names.

Many things you will find,
in a vast knowledge for the mind,
encyclopaedic they have to be,
Cigarette and Trade Cards, is the hobby for me.

From days of Empire, trade names shout out,
Vice Regal, Cornstalk and Hearts Delight,
Lucana and Scissors, Flag cigarettes too,
Wizard, Adventure, Radio Fun to name but a few.

Not just from England, you will find,
but many for the Chinese mind,
Australia, Malta, Holland too,
From German issues to Japan,
a truly *Global* view of man.

That sums it up,
do you not agree?
I am a *Cartophilist* without a degree . . .

Robert Christopher Cary

IN A TOY SHOP

I stop by a doorway and I look at the shop that
I pass each day,
it is a toy shop!
And then I reflect back on the days when I was young
and the lovely games I used to play.
I shyly open the door, I think for a while I will stay.

There are rows and rows of toys piled high
and I look at them and Gosh, how I sigh!
I pick up a teddy and hug it tight.
Fight these feeling! Why?
I will be a kid until I die.

And then thinking that I look around
and I listen to every single sound.
I see dads looking at boys' toys and oh, the look
on the elders faces of new found joys!,
an excuse to look at all the toys!.

I wander out the toy shop and hug the now
bought teddy.
And I smile and look about,
'Yes' we are all kids at heart . . .
without a doubt.

Susannah Rose Costello

I WISH I HAD A BOYFRIEND WITH A DECENT CAR

I wish I had a boyfriend with a decent car,
I'm not being too ungrateful,
it just doesn't get us far.

But it did get us on our hols, I have to be fair,
but with all the good intentions,
it broke down while we were there,
and I'd rather not, mention and try to forget,
and accident with a rabbit and a tree it closely met.

Then he bought a new red car,
there was hope and cheers of glee,
but oh,
how wrong someone could be.

But looking on the brighter side,
that red car's not too bad,
it's only had one fire,
and a crash it's never had.

It now has a new engine,
which is better than before,
and it never has been stolen,
of that! I can be sure.

But if I'm really honest,
and if I'm really true,
I wouldn't want to change him,
not for a new car or two,
and with our little adventures,
my life, would be so blue.

With all the love he gives me,
he makes my dreams complete,
which I try to remember,
when I'm in the passenger seat.

Rachel Firth

HOSPITAL CASUALTY

I was put in that casualty room
Cos' I hurt my toe using a broom
I was seeing the folk come and go
Little girls, little boys, Mr and Mrs So and So

Some had bad legs done in plaster
Nurse said come try walk a bit faster
A little girl was crying so much
She screamed and struggled and cried please Doc don't touch

It's an interesting place to be
In the Hospital Casualty
Then my name was called, come on Mr Brown
Now what was you doing with a broom in town

Well Doc I said I sweep up the road
When a big noise came and hit my toe
So they took a couple of X rays
Bruised, you'll be okay in a few days
Now go on be a good chap

Don't go and have another mishap
So everyone said goodbye to me
I was sorry to leave hospital casualty

J Christy

FOUR LEGGED LOVER

On whom do I focus my love,
on my dog! Is that really enough?
She's devoted to me. Guards and protects,
in return. Very little, she really expects.
I can do little else! 'but love' her, I feel.

She always keeps close, is not prone to stray
chases spiders and beetles, if they come her way.
When something's not right. Her bark tells me so!
loves visitors, friends. Doesn't want them to go.
I can do nothing else! 'but love' such a friend.

Affection and love, gentle 'kiss; on my legs.
When hanging the linen, she picks up the pegs.
Shakes with fright in the bath, and out tries to hop!
Treats me to a shower. As she shakes off the drops.
I can do little else! but love like she loves.

She squirms and protests, when her claws are just trimmed.
Her love never changes, her bright eyes, never dimmed
she's a friend and companion. Doesn't leave me alone,
is part of my life; and my house, and my home.
I can do nothing else! but love Sophie till death!

B Lenihan

TO A PET HERMIT

Shall I compare thee to a golden fish?
Thou ar't more hardened and preposterous,
you crawl about in thy small, glass-walled dish
which makes thee seem not all infesterous.
Thou has't the spirit of all crabs gone by
who, all too oft, were made into a feed,
but thy small jointed legs shall never fry,
instead thou shall maintain they crabby creed.
Though many pet crabs have met the dire fate
of having their tiny bodies trod,
thy small, shelled self shall never feel the weight
of some horribly, heavy human bod.
Though thy tiny claws may scratch and jab
I love you still my little hermit crab.

Karen Crawcour

DREAMS, HOPES AND HAPPINESS

I hear a voice, I hear a sound,
what is it that I have found?
Someone who cares, someone who will treat me
fair and always be there.
How have I come to deserve such kindness?
I'm eternally grateful that I have finally been able to find this.
So much happiness has started,
simply because these people are so kind-hearted.
People don't always see me for what I really am,
that's why I thought no-one gave a damn.
Now these people have showed me the truth,
and over ny head put a roof.
They understand exactly how I feel,
and they know that just like others my dreams
and hopes are for real!

Naomi Smith

147

REMEMBERING MOTHER

You loved the outdoor
the wild wind, the rain
now where do you roam,
your spirit is free,
no human body,
earthy chores, family?
Do you glide the glen
each day at dawn
your limbs again
as fleet as the faun.
Do you climb the hills
where rippling streams flow
with green mossy banks
where wild primrose grow?
I *feel* if you could
you would let me know.

Abina Russell

HOW MUCH I LOVE YOU

If you were in a wheelchair
If you could never walk again,
If you could never more love me physically,
I would feel just the same
As I do about you now you are in one piece,
I could never doubt you, my love will never cease
If your strong body was all broken
And your handsome face a mess.
I would gently kiss each scar
And count myself so blessed
To have ever held you -
To have been the woman you have desired,
You could never repulse me,
You would still fill me with fire.
If you should go on a drunken spree -
If your gentleness should change to wrath,
I would still be at your feet
Grateful for all we have had -
If you should yell 'Go away'
I will beg of you to let me stay.
So you see, my darling,
There is not one thing you can say or do
To stop me from caring,
For this is how much I love you.

Madeliene Eggleton

FROM US TO YOU

We arrive with feelings of dread,
Fearful thoughts of the ordeal ahead,
Smiles greet us as you show us to our beds,
Our troubles are eased with a nod of your head.

Your caring and patience to the ward you bring,
As once again our red bell we ring.
Personality, dedication is your lot,
Never wavering as the day grows hot.

You are our comforter and our prop,
From depression you lift us non stop.
Pulses and temperatures you take in the day,
Injections and dressings are too part of the fray.

Laughter and tears we give to you,
The brunt of our anger is yours too.
But never once do you lose your cool,
Later we realise we behaved like a fool.

You are our light in our hour of need,
As more tablets off you we plead.
Keep up the good work nurses dear,
Love from us all and cheers . . .

Jean Osborne

THE NEW BRUSH

This was a terrible place till I came
the patients were scruffy not just a few
The staff dead despondent decidedly blue
No forward planning and little was new
This was a right old shambles till I came

This is a wonderful place now I'm here
Eleven psychologists the philosophies tight
Patients Care Planning beginning to bite
Staff seasonal depression clean out of sight
We are totally committed now I'm here

It's a wunderbar place now I'm here
They don't seem to miss the wicked old booze
And I hardly find anyone having a snooze
Flowers are blooming there's bunf in the loos
Out every weekend on some meaningful cruise
This place is a credit now I'm here

This is a born again place now I'm here
But drat! I've been caught with my hand in the till
I hear my replacement coming over the hill
With a voice all hopeful, preggers and shrill
It's our tune I remember my eyes quickly fill
This was a terrible place till I came.

Judd Hulme

THE WOODMAN AND THE LARCH TREES

A plantation of Larch
Most pleasing to be seen
Ten acres, I would say
Brown trunks and branches, green
All in perfect lines
Which ever way you look
To what great pains
The woodman must have took.
Every tree like a soldier
Standing on parade.
The clever woodman knew this
When digging with his spade.
Surrounded by a sturdy fence
Oak post and oak rail
A centre stake
And a well driven nail.

The years will pass on
The Larch get wide and tall
Green needles into yellow, turn
And to the ground will fall.
The woodman knew this of course
When he planted them with care
He knew great trees they'd make
But he would not be there.

Keith Coleman

THE TRAMP

He walked along in solitude,
Shoulders drooped, reflecting his mood.
His coat was black, and very long,
To who? I wondered did he once belong.

His hair was black, yet fairly neat,
He had black boots, upon his feet.
His face was ashen, very pale,
He looked so gaunt, so very frail.

His belongings were carried in a plastic bag,
Tied around his waist, with a piece of rag.
His pointed beard, was flecked with grey,
What had made this man, turn out this way?

His eyes gave out a vacant look,
Seemed to ache with every step he took.
He didn't look to be very old,
Yet here he was, a man of the road.

Denise Sanders

A VISIT TO THE DENTIST

I walked into the bright clinically clean room.
I can't breathe, I'll have to go out soon.
My heart is thumping, stomach in knots tied.
My mind is saying 'I want to be outside'
What am I doing here today.
I'd sooner be anywhere far away.
'Come on in, please sit down'.
My legs won't move I feel such a clown.
Do I really need to have this extraction.
The pain has gone I'm torn to distraction.
'Open wide now let me see'
That one's the problem, most definitely.
I'm afraid it will have to come out.
I'm so nervous, I'm shaking I want to shout.
'I don't want to lose it is there another way'.
Perhaps I should leave it, I'll come back another day.
'No I'm sorry he replied'
'You're better off without this one inside'.
A little jab then you'll be alright.
My knuckles tightly clenched, and showing white.
Then it's gone, he's got it out.
What was all the fuss and panic about.
'There I told you, you'd feel no pain'
'Now you will come back in six months again?'
I feel elated as I head for the door.
Trying not to think about coming back in six months more.

Julie Guerin

THERE'S BONES DOWN THERE

A farmer's life can be tough
trying to cultivate his land that's rough
turning over the soil and many a stone
even on occasion some human bones
he gets off his tractor to investigate
as he draws near he hesitates
he realises a hole has appeared
but as he progresses near, it is as he feared
his worst nightmare has come true
he looks into the hole and blackened eyes peer through
he jumps up and runs away
only to notice his friends looking in dismay
he pulls himself together and goes back
heart pounding as if to have a heart attack
when he looks down the hole again
the colour of his panicked red face drains
off he goes to tell his boss
to make sure no time is lost
when the phone calls have been done
an investigation will have begun.
So the farmer leaves the field
knowing the crop for the future will not yield
another farming job he must go
for his tractor to fallow to and fro.

J A Burkill

AULD-FASHIONED GAMES

When did you last see weans playin' tig,
A game o' peever, or dancin' a jig?
Or a boy runnin' free wi' a cleek an' a gird?
    Long-too long ago!

In the spring o' the year, when the days grew bright
Oot cam' the bools that were long oot o' sight.
For steelies an' glessies ye played a' yer might.
    Long-too long ago!

Licht fit an' licht-herted on lang summer days,
The lassies at skippin' in intricate ways.
Plainie or Belgian, through ropes like a maze.
    Long-too long ago!

Where are the games o' yesteryear?
When enjoyment wis simple, the cost far fae dear,
And innocent pleasures, content wi' sma' gear.
    Long-too long ago!

Margaret M Osoba

THE BLIND MENDICANT

Horatious kept the Tiber Bridge
      he fought in days of yore.
Such a gallant feat of arms,
      ne'er was seen before.
But another man a bridge did keep,
      above the Tyne he stood
Blind at birth, he had to beg,
      hungering oft for food
With crippled arms, and shabby clothes
      oft times weary legged
He shivered cold in winter time
      yet he stayed and begged.
Pennies in his cup did fall,
      halfpennies, farthings too . . .
Many a day not fit to bed
      he carried on with flu'.
There was no social service pay
      he had to beg, or die.
Oft times knee deep in snow
      Poor Tommy did not cry.
One wonders where was God
      to ignore the poor man's plight
Seven he was, when first he begged
      upon High Level height.
Then when Swing Bridge was built,
      Tommy changed his stand . . .
For fifty year the poor Tommy begged
      in hopes of promised land
One winter storm, the wind did howl
      the snow did quickly fall
And poor blind Tommy, chilled to bone,
      could not raise a call.

They found him on the Gateshead shore
      lying in the snow,
Relatives, loved ones, there were none,
      to see this blind man go.

In union workhouse, Tommy died,
    his great fight was over.
In paupers grave that laid how low
    his flowers were only clover.
He'd fought the fight with all his might
    with courage, not a sword,
but if alas it should transpire
    no God in Heaven doth reign,
Then Tom, his body turned to earth,
    hath lived his life in vain.

Harold W Charlton

ABILITIES

Everyone has a latent talent
Lying dormant, not being apparent
Each one has an idealisation
Waiting to spring to manifestation

Some are shrewd and smart of strategy
Others being skilled in diplomacy
Each competent and efficient
With a vulpine slightly different

Those who are deft and inventive
Incessantly show their incentive
Being of natural ability
Demonstrate their capability

Blessed are those of versatility
Beneficially endowed of facility
Of all inadequacy they dispel
When they outshine and excel.

J F Wood

PERSISTENCE

Listen to the wind again
As it roars around the town,
Tearing at the window panes
And knocking chimneys down.
Rattling over rooftops
It rushes here and there,
Hurrying along the clouds above
And doesn't seem to care,
Bending trees right over
And breaking flowers so sweet,
Banging doors, and shaking bins
Rolling tin cans down the street,
Throwing dust up in my face
No mercy is it showing,
Tangles up my well groomed hair
Why does it keep on blowing?
It turns my brolly inside out
And nearly drives me crazy,
Oh, how I long for summer-time
When the days are long and hazy,
Listen to the wind again
As it roars with all its might,
Funny how it's always worse
When I'm trying to sleep at night!

June Scott

THE SMILE

A fleeting glance it was
Just by chance then she
Turned to smile at me,
I returned the smile trust
It were so nice to the lady
Fair with the straw
Coloured hair of that she
Gave to me.

I return each day searching
For the same,
Of that radiant smile
From the lady fair with
The straw coloured hair
Of that she gave to
Me.

I pray each night just
To catch the sight,
Of those sea green eyes
From the lady fair
With the straw coloured
Hair of that she
Gave to me.

Jim Hancock

FROM WAR TO ETERNITY

How many tears have fallen and, alas, how many broken hearts and broken
dreams?
The war is over, now the flotsum flows along uncharted shores amidst the
screams
For retribution: who can count the cost with many simple souls returning
lost?
And He who is the Piper asks for more, more effort, self-denial, sacrifice:
The war is over yet He still goes on, and those who heed the Piper pay
the price
For what they did and now for what they pledge and work the soil while
others trim the hedge.

The years go by and slowly, one by one, the veterans fade still cherishing
the flag:
The enemy becomes the one who lives next-door: the hero is the artist
dressed in drag,
And things of no importance magnify as Patriots draw the sword and
martyrs die.

Corruption and perversion now strip off to take the field with nothing
disallowed,
And figures that once tiptoes through the night are glamorised and jostled
by the crowd,
And drug abuse and child abuse become so commonplace, oh for the pipe
and drum.

When there is nothing left but rock and dust and time has done what man
had often dared:
When Hell and Heaven find no bones to pick, and emptiness marks where
a soldier shared
His finest hour, who'll reminisce on those who bled and fought and died . .
.

for this?

L Jeffries

THIS IS THE TRUTH?

An uncouth
Youth,
Fell from a roof,
Injuring his mouth.
To his dentist he flew,
Who -
Remaining aloof
Said he, to the youth:
'Come into my booth -
Open wide your mouth.'
As he peeped inside
He cried:
'Strewth!
I'm no sleuth,
But you've
Lost a tooth.
I can fix, at a cost
What you've lost.'
This story I can prove -
Believe me - forsooth!
For, I was that youth.
(He smiled giving me proof
Of his replaced tooth;
This price, costing not the earth,
Showed its worth).

Leonard Whitehead

INFORMATION

We hope you have enjoyed reading this book - and that you will continue to enjoy it in the coming years.

If you like reading and writing poetry drop us a line, or give us a call, and we'll send you a free information pack.

Write to

Anchor Books Information
1-2 Wainman Road
Woodston
Peterborough
PE2 7BU.